University Spatial Development and Urban Transformation in China

The past few decades have seen universities take on a leading role in urban development, actively providing public services beyond teaching and research. The relationship between the university and the city has great influence on the space of university, which is vividly reflected in the process of university spatial development. This process has been particularly evident in China as Chinese universities and cities have been undergoing dramatic transformations since reform in the late 1970s.

University Spatial Development and Urban Transformation in China explores the changing relationship between the university and the city from a spatial perspective. Based on theories and discourses on the production of space, the book analyzes case studies in university spatial development in China at three scales – global, national and local – covering social and urban contexts, the urban transformation, interactions in the development process and the changing dynamic between university and city to propose mutually beneficial planning strategies.

This book is a valuable resource for academics, researchers and urban planners in identifying the key factors and relationships in university spatial development using theoretical and empirical data to guide future urban planning.

Cui Liu is a lecturer in architecture and urban design at the College of Civil Engineering and Architecture, Zhejiang University, China, and a professional architect and urban planner.

Routledge Research in Planning and Urban Design
Series editor: Peter Ache
Radboud University, Nijmegen, Netherlands

Routledge Research in Planning and Urban Design is a series of academic monographs for scholars working in these disciplines and the overlaps between them. Building on Routledge's history of academic rigour and cutting-edge research, the series contributes to the rapidly expanding literature in all areas of planning and urban design.

www.routledge.com/Routledge-Research-in-Planning-and-Urban-Design/book-series/RRPUD

The Architecture of Phantasmagoria
Specters of the City
Libero Andreotti and Nadir Lahiji

Revolt and Reform in Architecture's Academy
William Richards

City Branding
The Politics of Representation in Globalising Cities
Alberto Vanolo

Urban Planning's Philosophical Entanglements
The Rugged, Dialectical Path from Knowledge to Action
Richard S. Bolan

Lost in the Transit Desert
Race, Transit Access and Suburban Form
Diane Jones Allen

University Spatial Development and Urban Transformation in China
Cui Liu

University Spatial Development and Urban Transformation in China

Cui Liu

Routledge
Taylor & Francis Group

LONDON AND NEW YORK

First published 2017
by Routledge
2 Park Square, Milton Park, Abingdon, Oxon OX14 4RN

and by Routledge
605 Third Avenue, New York, NY 10017

First issued in paperback 2022

Routledge is an imprint of the Taylor & Francis Group, an informa business

© 2017 Cui Liu

The right of Cui Liu to be identified as author of this work has
been asserted by her in accordance with sections 77 and 78 of the
Copyright, Designs and Patents Act 1988.

Publisher's Note
The publisher has gone to great lengths to ensure the quality of this reprint
but points out that some imperfections in the original copies may be apparent.

British Library Cataloguing-in-Publication Data
A catalogue record for this book is available from the British Library

Library of Congress Cataloging-in-Publication Data
Names: Liu, Cui (Architect), author.
Title: University spatial development and urban transformation in
    China / Cui Liu.
Description: New York : Routledge, 2017. | Series: Research in
    planning and urban design | Includes bibliographical references.
Identifiers: LCCN 2017006855 | ISBN 9781138232402 (hb) |
    ISBN 9781315312651 (ebook)
Subjects: LCSH: City planning—Social aspects—China. | Space
    (Architecture)—China. | Community and college—China. |
    Knowledge management—China.
Classification: LCC HT169.C6 L56 2017 | DDC 307.1/
    2160951—dc23
LC record available at https://lccn.loc.gov/2017006855

ISBN 13: 978-1-03-240214-7 (pbk)
ISBN 13: 978-1-138-23240-2 (hbk)
ISBN 13: 978-1-315-31265-1 (ebk)

DOI: 10.4324/9781315312651

Typeset in Times New Roman
by Apex CoVantage, LLC

Contents

PART III
Case studies 95

Figures

Tables

Acknowledgements

This book is largely based on my doctoral research, carried out at the Polytechnic of Milan's PhD program of Spatial Planning and Urban Development, and it has been greatly improved with fresh ideas during my latest studies. I want to give my sincere gratitude to my doctorate supervisor, Professor Valeria Fedeli, for her inspiring advice and consistent encouragement. I owe heartfelt thanks to Professor Alessandro Balducci, who led me into this field of research and provided valuable suggestions at important points of my career. My genuine thanks extend to Professors Costanzo Ranci, Luca Gaeta, Corrina Morandi, Gabriele Pasqui, Stefano Moroni, Luisa Pedrazzini, Marco Ponti, Luigi Mazza, Remo Dorigati and Antonella Bruzzese who enriched my knowledge through insightful lectures and conversations.

During my earlier internship at the Great Cities Institute of University of Illinois at Chicago, Professor David Perry helped me clarify some concepts that are crucial to my research. More recently, Professor Yuzhuo Cai from University of Tampere has given me important guidance on exploring new ideas and publishing the works. I have benefited a lot from their words of wisdom and I hope this work is in itself some reward.

Warm thanks to my friends Yu Liu, Funda Atun, Rositsa Ilieva, Matilde Cassani, Emanuela Saporito and Enrico Tommarchi, for spending endless hours with me brainstorming and putting forward justifiable criticism, and to my colleagues at Zhejiang University who are always willing to share with me their knowledge, skills, passions and experiences on work and life. I am deeply indebted to my family for always being there for me, through life's excitement and sorrow, and providing me unconditional support and unending encouragement whenever I need help.

Thanks also to Sade Lee and Grace Harrison for their editorial assistance and to the anonymous reviewer of the book for his/her suggestions.

My earlier doctorate research was supported by the Chinese Scholarship Council and the recent further studies were supported by National Natural Science Foundation of China (Grant No. 51508497).

Cui Liu

China

October 2016

Introduction

Mutual influence of universities and cities in the knowledge society

Today it is taken for granted that knowledge is the real and valuable resource that can change the world day by day (Drucker, 1993; Lundvall & Johnson, 1994; Nonaka, 1991; Powell & Snellman, 2004). The growth of the knowledge economy has prompted the expansion of universities, increased their local influence, and brought attention to their ability of raising regional competitiveness (Charles, 2006). The universities are expected not only to cultivate intellectuals through educating students and training people already in work, but also perform as knowledge-producing and disseminating institutions that will directly lead to technology transfer and innovation (Etzkowitz & Leydesdorff, 2000; Lundvall, 2002; Rutten, Boekema, & Kuijpers, 2003; Slaughter & Rhoades, 2004). Furthermore, the universities are expected to play a civic role in nation building by promoting a positive and progressive public culture (Chatterton, 2000; Florida, 2002; Readings, 1996). All in all, the universities are increasingly playing an important and even a leading role in urban development.

As the hosting place of universities, the cities are gradually transformed by the increasing calls for the engagement of universities in bringing their intellectual and institutional resources into their immediate environment. The prospering of universities changes the territorial organization of land uses and the linkages between them; it has direct influence on the local land market and housing market, and provides a potential for labour reallocation (Perry & Wiewel, 2005; Wiewel & Perry, 2008). The university-led innovation helps to technology transfer and promotes the urban economic restructuring based on knowledge creation (Florax, 1992). Moreover, deeply rooted in the place, the development of the universities involves actors with diverse interests, thus becoming a contesting stage of various urban powers (van der Wusten, 1998). Besides, the massification of higher education also sheds light on the university's role in nurturing a civic community for the cities (Balducci, Cognetti, & Fedeli, 2010). Thus the engagement of universities in urban development becomes a solid factor of competitive advantage for the cities.

The mutual influence of the university and the city involves not only the extensive physical fabric of the university with its facilities, premises and public spaces, but also the people who populate it, such as the students, faculties and host communities, as well as the activities that such groups undertake and the associating economic and social impacts. All of these spatial orientations and practices, the relations and orders established, and the underpinning culturally embedded assumptions and symbolism are vividly reflected in the production process of the space (Lefebvre, 1991). Thus the space of university is an active field to examine the interaction between the university and the city. University spatial development shows the role of the university in the context of dynamic urban transformation, and it also explains well the process of urban transformation in the knowledge society.

Key questions

This book is going to explore the mechanism of university–city interaction in the knowledge society from a spatial perspective. It is guided by the following questions:

- What are the social and urban contexts for university spatial development?
- How is the space of university developed and how do the university and the city interact with each other in this process?
- How is the city transformed and how are university–city relations changed due to university spatial development?

The book aims to explore the dynamics of university spatial development and urban transformation and the mechanism of their interrelations, to identify the tensions and barriers of university–city interaction, and to propose spatial strategies for mutually beneficial university–city relations.

Methodology

There are three steps in the book to explore the mechanism of university–city interaction: 1) interpretation on the space of the university from the spatial, temporal and social perspectives, which sets up the background of the book in the Chinese context and the knowledge society; 2) analysis on the dynamics of university spatial development and urban transformation and their interactive relationships at the global, national and local scales; 3) case studies on two university sites in Shanghai, which represent different types of university–city interaction.

Cross-dimensional interpretation

The understanding of the space of university is conducted from two sets of dimensions: spatio-temporal and socio-spatial. The spatio-temporal perspective is embedded in the Chinese context. By examining the evolution of Chinese universities, especially the changing social values of the university and the related changes in space, it provides some historical clues for understanding contemporary university spatial practices in China. The socio-spatial perspective focuses on the interrelations between the space and society along with the rise of the knowledge economy. It is guided by the theories about the production of space and discusses the meaning of the space of the university in the knowledge society by viewing it as the material product of society, the manifestation of social relations and the means of social production. The spatio-temporal and socio-spatial perspectives contribute to a comprehensive understanding of the space of university.

Multi-scale coding matrix

Analysis on the mechanism of university–city interaction is carried out at three scales, i.e. the global, the national and the local scales. The production of scale is implied in the production of space (Cox, 1998). It is clear to see the university as a point situated in the space defined by the local and global axes, a spatial sphere where localized social relations depend and where global knowledge producers engage. This book also introduces the national scale of China as an intermediary between the global and the local. It does not select the regional or super-national scale because the national scale of China reflects the social struggle for power and control most obviously. The analytical framework in the book extends from the abstract social process in the globalization process, through the institutional restructuring in China's national reform, to the urban socio-economic restructuring in the city of Shanghai. The global, national and local scales are related, interpenetrating, and frequently influence each other. Analysis at any single scale could not explain the overall complexity of university spatial development. They are separated in the research just to facilitate the analytical expression and not to mean their absolute distinction in nature.

The book uses a coding paradigm (Strauss & Corbin, 1998) to sort out and organize the emerging connections at each scale. The basic components of the coding paradigm include conditions, actions/interactions and consequences. Conditions form the structure or set of circumstances or situations in which the university–city interaction is embedded. It is a conceptual way of grouping answers to the research question 'what are the social and urban contexts for university spatial development'. Actions/interactions are strategic or routine responses made by the university and other related actors to the issues, problems, happenings or events that arise under those conditions. They are represented by the research question 'how is the space of university developed and how do the university and the city interact with each other in this process'. Consequences are outcomes of the actions and interactions. They are represented by the research question 'how is the city transformed and how are university-city relations changed due to university spatial development'.

The coding paradigm is aimed to capture the mechanism and the complex nature of the university–city interaction. It is not for terms such as conditions, actions/interactions and consequences by placing data into discrete boxes. In fact, the paradigm is nothing more than a perspective taken toward data and an analytical stance that helps to systematically gather and order data in such a way that structure and process are integrated. Neither is the coding paradigm a language of cause and effect. Identifying, sifting through, and sorting through all of the possible factors showing the nature of the relationships does not result in a simple 'if . . . then' statement. The result is much more likely to be a discussion that takes readers along a complex path of interrelationships, each in its own patterned way that explains what is going on. The multi-scale modeling together with the coding paradigm constitutes the analytical matrix of the book.

Case study

This book is embedded in the Chinese context and adopts the city of Shanghai as an example with two sites as sub-units, Songjiang University Town and Tongji Creative Cluster. It is set in the Chinese context because it has been commonly perceived that China is now increasingly involved in the new global space of higher education, not only in terms of the large quantity of students abroad but also regarding the frequent collaboration with foreign universities as well as active engagement in international academic fields (Altbach & Umakoshi, 2004; Breton & Lambert, 2003; Lambert & Butler, 2006). However, there is still insufficient research on the role of Chinese universities in triggering social transformation from a global point of view.

The book selects Shanghai as an example because, as China's largest metropolis, Shanghai is the most obvious contesting place of various forces driving urban transformation, especially to examine the momentum of the universities in promoting the knowledge-based global economy, given that

Shanghai is the second city in China with the largest number of universities. Moreover, taking Shanghai as an example provides a comparative and revelatory case for other global cities on how to better incorporate universities into the urban development strategy to promote urban competitiveness in the knowledge society.

The book focuses on the two university sites, Songjiang University Town and Tongji Creative Cluster, because they represent two different typical modes of university spatial development in China. Songjiang University Town is a top-down strategy to promote urbanization through university agglomerations and, at the same time, to meet the requirement of university expansion and to facilitate resource sharing and cooperation between universities. Tongji Creative Cluster is originated spontaneously from the spillover effect of the university and is used to lead the urban renewal process of its surrounding areas. The university, government and industry play quite different roles in the two cases. The book includes the two cases as subunits of the city level instead of a downward scale because the key actors in the two cases do not enjoy much autonomy in policy-making but are largely subject to the management of municipal institutions.

The case study was conducted on the basis of literature review and fieldwork. The dataset, in addition to some academic publications, mainly includes laws, official policies and planning documents obtained from official websites, relevant newspapers and other reliable sources such as internal communications. The fieldwork includes interviews with university leaders, enterprise employees, planners, local inhabitants, teachers and students. Personal connections were used to contact some of the initial interviewees, and those then suggested other relevant informants from among their acquaintances, following the 'snowball' technique. The interviewees were either asked the same questions to compare and analyze their varying roles and relations, or asked questions that were closely related to their specific roles. The interviews were generally conducted at interviewees' workplaces, and varied in length from 30 to 60 minutes. Other informal interviews were also conducted on different occasions, such as in bookshops and restaurants around the university. Most of the informal talks were short, but they complement and balance the data collected through formal interviews.

Overview of the book

The book consists of nine chapters and is divided into three major parts besides the opening and the ending chapters.

Chapter 1 and 2 are the first major part of the book, providing cross-dimensional understanding of the space of universities. Chapter 1 provides a spatio-temporal review on the evolution of universities in Chinese history. It discusses the various university models at different historical periods of China, explores the embedding ideologies and social values, and identifies the spatial characteristics of different university models.

Chapter 2 provides a socio-spatial perspective on the role of the university in the knowledge society. It discusses the meaning of the space of university in the concrete aspect (university as knowledge infrastructure in the knowledge society), the abstract aspect (university as the contesting stage of social relations) and the instrumental aspect (university engagement in urban/regional development).

Chapter 3, 4 and 5 are the second major parts of the book, exploring the dynamics of university spatial development and urban transformation at the global, national and local scales. Chapter 3 analyzes the mechanism of university spatial development in the globalizing world. It examines the changing global space of the urban universities by exploring the key factors of innovation system and global urban competitiveness in the knowledge society, the urban strategies to promote urban competitiveness, the requirements on and the responses of universities, the changing geography of global university networks, and the strategic importance of global universities to global cities.

Chapter 4 analyzes the interaction between universities and cities in the process of Chinese reform. It first discusses the changing state governance in China characterized by decentralization and marketization; then examines the related influence on urban development strategies and practices; next it focuses on the urban needs on higher education and the restructuring of university governance into local plans; after that it explores the role of universities in the Chinese innovation system; finally it analyzes changing university–city relations and the underpinning values.

Chapter 5 explores changing university–city relations in the process of Shanghai's urban social–economic restructuring and urban spatial restructuring. It discusses the urban development patterns of Shanghai in the post-reform era, the increasing importance of higher education in the urban socio-economic restructuring, the measures of university expansion along with the massification of higher education, the engagement of universities in urban spatial restructuring, and the challenges to the concept of urban university.

Chapter 6 and 7 are the third major parts of the book, approaching the mechanism of university–city interaction through case studies. Chapter 6 is about the case study on Songjiang University Town. It begins with the urban strategy on the satellite city of Songjiang and the fostering of the university town as a catalyst project; then it discusses the governance coalitions and the implementation of the ideal plan; after that it specifies the influence of the university town on the real estate market, industrialization and urbanization.

Chapter 7 is about the case study on Tongji Creative Cluster. It discusses the evolution of Tongji Creative Cluster from a spontaneous agglomeration to a national science park, the role of the key actors such as the university, the government and enterprises in promoting the development of the Cluster, the driving forces and the development models of the Cluster at different stages, and the geographical, economical and institutional contribution of the Cluster to the urban district.

The last chapter is the concluding chapter. It makes a summary about the mechanism of university–city interaction in response to the research questions, examines the tensions and barriers in the university–city interaction, and proposes spatial strategies for mutually beneficial university–city relations.

References

Altbach, P. G., & Umakoshi, T. (Eds.). (2004). *Asian Universities: Historical Perspectives and Contemporary Challenges*. Baltimore, MD: Johns Hopkins University Press.

Balducci, A., Cognetti, F., & Fedeli, V. (Eds.). (2010). *Milano, la città degli studi. Storia, geografia e politiche delle università milanesi*. Milan: Abitare Segesta Cataloghi.

Breton, G., & Lambert, M. (Eds.). (2003). *Universities and Globalization: Private Linkages, Public Trust*. Paris: UNESCO.

Charles, D. (2006). Universities as key knowledge infrastructures in regional innovation systems. *Innovation the European Journal of Social Science Research, 19*(1), 117–130.

Chatterton, P. (2000). The cultural role of universities in the community: Revisiting the university – community debate. *Environment & Planning A, 32*(1), 165–181.

Cox, K. R. (1998). Spaces of dependence, spaces of engagement and the politics of scale, or: Looking for local politics. *Political Geography, 17*(1), 1–23.

Drucker, P. (1993). *Post-Capitalist Society*. New York: Harper Business.

Etzkowitz, H., & Leydesdorff, L. (2000). The dynamics of innovation: From National Systems and "Mode 2" to a Triple Helix of university – industry – government relations. *Research Policy, 29*(2), 109–123.

Florax, R. J. G. M. (1992). *The University: A Regional Booster?: Economic Impacts of Academic Knowledge Infrastructure*. Aldershot: Avebury.

Florida, R. (2002). *The Rise of the Creative Class*. New York: Basic Books.

Lambert, R., & Butler, N. (2006). *The Future of European Universities: Renaissance or Decay?* London: Centre for European Reform.

Lefebvre, H. (1991). *The Production of Space* (D. Nicholsonsmith, Trans.). Oxford and Cambridge: Blackwell Publishers.

Lundvall, B. Å. (2002). The University in the Learning Economy. *Druid Working Papers*.

Lundvall, B. Å., & Johnson, B. (1994). The learning economy. *General Information, 1*(2), 23–42.

Nonaka, I. (1991). The knowledge-creating company. *Harvard Business Review, 69*(6), 96–104.

Perry, D., & Wiewel, W. (Eds.). (2005). *The University as Urban Developer: Case Studies and Analysis*. Armonk: M. E. Sharpe.

Powell, W. W., & Snellman, K. (2004). The knowledge economy. *Annual Review of Sociology, 30*(1), 199–220.

Readings, B. (1996). *The University in Ruins*. Cambridge: Harvard University Press.

Rutten, R., Boekema, F., & Kuijpers, E. (Eds.). (2003). *Economic Geography of Higher Education: Knowledge Infrastructure and Learning Regions*. New York: Routledge.

Slaughter, S., & Rhoades, G. (2004). *Academic Capitalism and the New Economy: Markets, State, and Higher Education*. Baltimore: The Johns Hopkins University Press.

Strauss, A. L., & Corbin, J. M. (1998). *Basics of Qualitative Research: Techniques and Procedures for Developing Grounded Theory*. London: Sage.

van der Wusten, H. (Ed.). (1998). *The Urban University and Its Identity: Roots, Locations, Roles*. Dordrecht: Kluwer Academic Publishers.

Wiewel, W., & Perry, D. (Eds.). (2008). *Global Universities and Urban Development: Case Studies and Analysis*. New York: M. E. Sharpe, Lincoln Institute of Land Policy.

Part I

The spatial, temporal and social perspectives

1 The evolution of universities in Chinese history

Spatio-temporal perspectives

The university is not a new-born thing. It has a history of over 3,000 years in China. The space of university is transforming over time as guided by a wide variety of social values. There were practices to revive traditional higher education institutions, to establish Western missionary universities, to orient university for productive use, to blend the university into everyday life, to mobilize the university for social revolution and so on. In the modern era, the indigenous tradition of higher education in China was mixed with various exotic academic models such as the European, American and Soviet models. Those at the present time might be of different order from those of the earlier period. However, it can be considered to a certain degree that the space of university today is influenced and governed by its historical links. History gives us some hints on the evolution of the space of university and about how to make the space of university a productive one. This chapter will examine the features of the space of university, their interaction with the city and the society, and their underlying social values in different historical periods of China.

Indigenous scholarly institutions

Chinese higher education originated as early as in 1100 B.C. during the Zhou dynasty and was called *pi-yong*. During the Han dynasty (206 B.C. – A.D. 220), higher education institutions were called *tai-xue*, which means 'institutions of higher learning', and were attended by more than 30,000 students during the dynasty's most prosperous time at its main campus in the capital city Chang'an (Wang et al., 2007). During the Tang dynasty (A.D. 618–907) and afterward, Chinese universities were called *guo-zi-jian*, a type of higher education institutions established for the children of royal families and senior officials. The content of learning was drawn from the classical texts of Confucian teachings, which were also the dominant contents of the imperial examinations for senior civil service positions.

In addition to these ancient universities established by the Chinese state, which continued to exist until the late nineteenth century, private universities also flourished in ancient China. Confucius (551–479 B.C.) introduced private higher education in China during the Eastern Zhou dynasty, at a time when state institutions were becoming weaker (Min, 2004). And it was recorded that Confucius had taught more than 3,000 students. It became fashionable to run private learning institutions during that time, and many leading scholars at different schools operated their own institutions. There were also professional schools for law, medicine, mathematics, literature and calligraphy studies.

When speaking of ancient scholarly institutions of higher learning, one must mention *shu-yuan*. These institutions started to appear during the Tang dynasty (A.D. 618–907), when they were first established in both the state and private sectors as places for collecting books. Initially *Shu-yuan* were not places for teaching and learning but they gradually developed into private academies or scholarly societies, as alternatives to official higher education institutions. Their studies were not limited to the orthodox definition of knowledge institutionalized in the imperial examinations, but introduced new currents of thought drawn from Buddhism, Daoism and other sources. Influenced by liberalism embedded in these thoughts, *shu-yuan* were usually built away from cities or towns, providing a quiet environment where scholars could engage in studies and contemplation without restrictions and worldly distractions. Closely combined with the charming scenery in the natural environment, *shu-yuan* became a special cultural landscape, with flexible and idyllic spatial patterns.

While largely independent and often financed by private endowments of land, *shu-yuan* tended to rise and decline in accordance with the quality and vision of the great scholars who singly headed them up (Hayhoe, 1989), and they were constantly under threat from the imperial bureaucracy that sought to co-opt them to the service of the examination system or destroy them in some periods. In the Song dynasty (960–1279 A.D), the Confucian classics were reordered to form a knowledge system that had to be mastered by all aspiring to become scholar-officials in the imperial civil service. Hanlin Academy, an official institute of the state, regulated the interpretation and application of the classical texts. The imperial examination system thus dominated traditional higher education, creating a class of intellectuals who climbed the ladder of a series of examinations to become officials (Miyazaki, 1971).

Therefore, *shu-yuan* were gradually moved from the suburb to the city with the control of the government to serve for the imperial dominance. After the Jiading period (1208–1225), large numbers of *shu-yuan* were established in the central cities. Worship, a traditional ceremony in the

Chinese imperial system, became a constant activity in *shu-yuan* besides its traditional functions in collecting books and teaching. The spatial layout of formalized *shu-yuan* in the imperial examination system was changed accordingly. The previous relatively free organization of buildings was replaced by formalized and ritual rules, although the idyllic ideal was still preserved in the layout of landscape. Palaces and temples appeared in *shu-yuan* for worship; examination halls and shooting gardens were established to select both civil and military elites. The donation and funding of the government became the main financial sources for *shu-yuan*. The bestowal of a calligraphic signboard by the Emperor became an extremely important symbol of an academy's status.

In fact, *shu-yuan* of traditional China may be a closer parallel to the medieval universities in Europe. Both of them were originated in feudal society and held the educational philosophy of elitism. Their campuses were enclosed in a courtyard integrating the activities of teaching, research and daily life altogether. However, the different history and culture generated different value system. Traditional universities in China never had the kind of statutory group autonomy enjoyed by the medieval universities through their papal charters (Hayhoe, 1989). The Chinese imperial bureaucracy enjoyed a scholarly monopoly and authority over the intellectual community, which was never effectively challenged until the empire itself began to crumble.

Universities in search of modernity

Although the indigenous tradition had a significant impact on the Chinese higher education system, modern Chinese universities developed from the European model, with a wistful longing for the *shu-yuan* tradition from time to time. This process involved a long and even painful interaction with the West after the Opium War in 1840, which made Chinese intellectuals aware of Western advances in science and technology and of the backwardness of China. This period was the most active and fertile stage in Chinese history to explore the university development modes.

Western missionary universities

When Western missionaries first found themselves able to operate with considerable freedom on Chinese soil, their primary concern was direct evangelism. But since Christian and traditional Chinese culture held different values, the missionaries met great opposition in their religious mission. After years of struggle, the missionaries realized that people's resistance could only be devolved through a compromise with the Confucian ideology, a feasible way of which was to call on the upper ruling strata and the intelligentsia to influence ordinary people. Therefore, some missionaries began to pay attention to the interrelation between the civilization of Chinese society and the spread of the Gospel.

A gradual thought in their minds was to introduce Western university models. Many foreign groups tried to create universities in China, including French Jesuit missionaries, American Protestants with the cooperation of British and Canadian colleagues, and German industrialists (Hayhoe, 1987). Catholics began to focus on developing parochial education to teach new converts basic religious and liturgical knowledge. Protestant missionaries turned to medical and educational work when they faced difficulties and discouragement in their evangelical efforts. Nearly all of the missionary universities were located in the foreign concessions inside key cities that became treaty ports, following the legal jurisdictions of their homeland countries. To localize themselves in China, the missionary universities tried to combine the Western approach with Chinese style in university planning. The campus was divided into several functional zones according to Western principles, with traditional Chinese gardens going across the zones and connecting them into an integral whole.

The western university models introduced by missionaries into China were embedded with great ambitions. The mission of these colleges was oriented towards political and cultural goals rather than simply religious ones. Their value lied in the long-term guarantee of foreign interests in China through the control of education and intellectuals. These institutions were very attractive to young Chinese intellectuals after the imperial examination system was abolished in China in 1905, and their graduates contributed to the modernization of nearly all areas, such as law, engineering and medicine in ways that were limited by the inherent conservatism and respect for authority of the Jesuit order. For example, law graduates from l'Universit l'Aurore, a French Catholic university established by French Jesuits in 1903 in Shanghai, advised the Nationalist government on legal reforms along French lines and supporting French imperialist insistence so that France's extra-territorial privileges should not be revoked until an 'acceptable' modern Chinese legal system had been established (Hayhoe, 1987).

By 1949, there were 21 universities run or subsidized by foreigners (Min, 2004), including such influential institutions as Yenching University in Beijing (the later Peking University) and St. Johns University in Shanghai (the later Tongji University). Among the total of 205 universities in the country, foreign universities accounted for about 10% and enrolled about 10,000 students (Wang et al., 2007). The universities that were established by the missionaries and other foreign groups had contributed greatly to the economic and political exploitation of foreign forces in China and exerted deep influence on the development of modern higher education in China. But they were still largely peripheral to the mainstream education reforms being engineered by a modernizing Chinese leadership.

Conservative modernization efforts

For Chinese modernizers of the late Qing dynasty and early republican periods, the missionary institutions were minor irritants in a situation where their own conception of higher education reform clearly reflected the political vision of each period. They did not look to missionary efforts for inspiration in their reforms, but visited or sent delegations to the nations whose educational institutions were of interest and modelled their reforms directly on foreign experience (Hayhoe, 1989). In 1847, three young students went to the United States for university studies, the first Chinese to do so. In 1872, the Chinese government decided to send a group of 120 students to the United States, initiating the country's first official study-abroad programs. This was followed by programs that sent students to the United Kingdom and continental European countries. In the wake of increased Japanese influence in China, many Chinese scholars and students went to Japan, where they experienced the European university model with a Japanese imprint (Min, 2004). A large proportion of the returned students worked in the Chinese higher education system as teachers, researchers and administrators, becoming a driving force in the development of Chinese universities.

One of the modernization efforts introduced in China after the Opium War was the movement to adapt the Western university model and to promote the learning of Western science and technology as a response to foreign aggression. From the 1860s to the 1880s, Western-style military and naval academies and foreign-language institutions were established by the powerful scholar–officials in China to train young people capable of dealing with the barbarians at both a diplomatic and military level. These institutions were strictly subordinate to the traditional institutions of the imperial examination system and the *shu-yuan*, which continued to focus on the classical knowledge tradition. And they were confident that Western technologies could be absorbed into a revitalized Confucian empire to deal effectively with foreign incursions. These thoughts were evident in the fact that some Western missionaries were appointed to leadership positions within the government-opened foreign language institutions and were trusted to develop Western studies that would contribute to China's self-strengthening (Hayhoe, 1989).

Therefore, universities at this time did not get rid of the pursuit of scholarly officials in traditional *shu-yuan* and did not understand the spirit of freedom and democracy in European universities, but were still government-controlled higher education institutions. The space of the universities followed the typical organization of *shu-yuan*, making only minor changes to adapt themselves to the changed educational and social requirement. For example, the form of formalized *shu-yuan* that was characterized by ritualized building groups and artistic natural landscape was reserved for teaching the traditional courses; physical environment as required by modern higher education was organized along a sub-axis parallel to the main traditional ritual axis. Moreover, the spatial organization no longer followed the model of traditional Chinese courtyard but a Western model of squares with relatively open borders enclosed by buildings.

However, it was not anticipated that most students abroad got access to the radical and revolutionary currents of thought rather than those supportive of the gradualist reform envisaged by their mentors in China. Neither was it expected that the translation of scientific and social materials by the liberally minded missionaries was a powerful source of new ideas for Chinese reformers who became more and more radical in their demands. Likewise in China itself, the real educational progress of the period was achieved less by the official public institutions than by the energetic gentry who set up their own modern schools (Hayhoe, 1989). By 1910 there were only three universities established by the imperial government. Most part of modern higher education was carried out in gentry-supported colleges, provincial higher institutions and missionary colleges.

Radical education reform

With the Revolution of 1911, the provisional government established by Sun Yat Sen in Nanjing appointed Cai Yuanpei as Minister of Education. In the higher education legislation of 1912, Cai introduced a European model derived largely from the German universities of Berlin and Leipzig where he had studied between 1908 and 1911. The aims of education formulated by Cai and expressed in the 1912 legislation were five-fold: utilitarian, moral, military, aesthetic and a world view. Cai saw the first three as essential to republican political and economic development, while the latter two rose above politics and were to foster a modern Chinese spirit that would replace Confucianism. While the higher professional institutions were to be largely committed to utilitarian, moral and military education, Cai felt that the universities had a special responsibility for aesthetic education as a bridge to build a modern Chinese world view. By emulating the German model with its central values of autonomy, professorial self-government and academic freedom, he succeeded in creating what was probably the first truly modern Chinese university, which provided the context for the May 4th movement in 1919, a movement whose cultural and political implications constituted an important turning point for modern China.

The space of university under such influences showed typical features of openness, freedom and diversity. The university shared its educational and cultural resources with the city, while the city performed certain social functions as the university. University planning did not restrict to the Western style or the Chinese character, neither was it aimed to build a totally new world as pursued by Western missionaries. What took into consideration by modern reformers was just actual needs and social reality. It followed economic principles. The university encouraged free interaction between the students and teachers as well as between the university and the community and provided space to facilitate such activities. For example, campus walls in some universities were cancelled in order to open the university to society; campus buildings were organized around the courtyards to form some small venues; the residence of students and teachers were located near to each other. Modern educationists paid high value to traditional Chinese culture and kept both the ritual layout of buildings and the idyllic ideal of landscapes in campus design.

Universities with nationalistic spirits

With the accession of the Nationalist Party to power in 1927, China finally had a clearly focused modern ideology in Sun Yat-sen's Three Principles of the People: nationalism, people's livelihood and people's rights. The tutelage of the Party was regarded as essential before people's rights could be fully implemented, and education was aimed to serve economic development and nationalistic unity. The Nationalist government imposed order on higher education by new legislation and hierarchical bureaucracy. The national universities were administered and funded by the central Ministry of Education in Nanjing, while the provincial-level institutions were managed by the provincial higher education bureaus. Clear regulations were given for the control of private institutions through an external board of governors whose organization and powers were overseen by the Ministry of Education (Ministry of Education of China, 1947). By June of 1931 there were 39 universities, 17 colleges and 23 professional schools in China (Zhou, 2007).

Cai's ideal about the university as an autonomous, self-governing and free scholarly institution was frustrated. But he still strived to add the French pattern of a university council to the German model that he previously introduced. It was envisaged by Cai to provide intellectuals the needed context for disinterested scholarly research under the umbrella of the council. In 1927, a National University Council was organized to take the lead in a geographical and curricular rationalization of higher education, which would ensure one major university in each region to supervise all other levels of education in the district. But unfortunately the National University Council was not aimed for Cai's vision of a modern Chinese university standing above politics, but was actually manipulated to better supervise the regional universities and all other levels of education in the district so as to harness them to economic and nationalistic purposes. Meanwhile, attempts to implement the university district scheme in many provinces met fierce opposition both from the universities determining to maintain their independent identity and from the lower echelons of education whose leaders did not see a scholarly control of education as supportive of their interests. Moreover, although the National University Council was aimed for the geographical rationalization of higher education, the distribution of universities was largely uneven, partly due to the influence of war and partly by uneven national development. Of the 15 national universities and colleges, nine were found in three east coast cities (Beijing, Nanjing and Shanghai), which also had 19 of the 27 private universities and colleges; three other cities (Tianjin, Chengdu and Taiyuan) had nine of the 18 provincial universities and colleges (Hayhoe, 1989).

Later, during the period of Chiang Kai-shek (1928–1949), education was even promoted to restore classic culture and to consolidate the one-party dictatorship. Confucian morality and norms were worshipped and indigenous Chinese tradition was popular again, which was most explicitly reflected in the planning of Sichuan University. Different from most universities at that time, Sichuan University was not established in the urban fringe, but located in the urban centre and developed on the basis of the ruined imperial palace, which was considered to symbolize Chinese traditional culture most distinctively (Chen, 2008). The main public buildings of the university, such as the auditorium, the library, the teaching buildings and the staff club, were arranged in the foreside of the main axis; the buildings of various departments were located on the sides of the main axis; the living areas of students and staff were concentrated in the rear of the campus. Such a kind of spatial layout followed exactly the organization principles of the imperial palace; namely the Outer Court or Front Court was used for ceremonial purposes, while the Inner Court or Back Palace functioned as the residence of the Emperor and his family and the place of dealing with the daily affairs. A series of courtyards were connected with each other along the vertical axis in the Front Court and extended horizontally in the Back Palace.

Communist revolutionary universities

The revolutionary institutions created by the Chinese Communist Party were perhaps the only modern higher education institutions in China that were created in conscious rejection of all the foreign models (Huang, Shi, &

Zhang, 1984). Shanghai University, the earliest institution owned by the Communist Party, provided programs in fine arts, literature and social science for Shanghai workers and students between 1922 and 1928 before it was forcibly closed by the Nationalist government. Its scholars scorned the empty theorizing of many universities and condemned them for their aping without grasping the substance of Western ideas. Qu Qiubai, an early and distinguished Communist thinker and leader of the university's sociology department, promoted a Chinese sociology that should arise from the active theoretical and practical engagement of Chinese scholars in the revolutionary transformation of China's patriarchal societal patterns.

With the move from a worker-based to a peasant-based revolutionary movement, a different type of higher education institutions was created by the Chinese Communist Party, first in Jiangxi soviet region and later in Yan'an and other border regions. They were set up in a studied independence from the Soviet models which were thought unsuited to the conditions of the Chinese Revolution. The Anti-Japanese Resistance University was established as a short-term training school for military cadres. It won some of its reputation from the fact that some major revolutionary figures such as Mao Zedong lectured there and in the course of their lectures came out some of the applied social science that contributed to revolutionary success. This gave it a special prestige and probably led to its revival as a model of educational reform during the Cultural Revolution period (1966–1976).

In the communist revolutionary universities, the working class were regarded as the primary educators as well as the main educational objects. There was a close link between education and labour with the aim to serve the revolution and class struggle. The universities discarded the disciplinary organization and highlighted the open, informal and practical principles in education. The students and teachers were in the public spotlight while the campus was just auxiliary and blended with the social, more exactly, the rural environment. The informal approach to teaching and learning and the strong student engagement in administration and self-government echoed some values of the earlier *shu-yuan* tradition. On the other side, the courses were mainly about political thought and military techniques with the aim to cultivate cadres for the communist government. There were also explicit administrative hierarchies in the organization of universities. The communist universities were notably integrated into the Border Region bureaucracy and were more like political institutions rather than academic institutions.

Soviet academic influence

With their access to power, the Chinese Communist Party differed little from the Nationalists in viewing higher education entirely within their new political vision. All the educational institutions were nationalized and became state-run institutions (Tsang, 2000). It was totally different from the higher education system before 1949 in which the development of the public, private and missionary universities were independent from each other. In contrast, the planning and financing of higher education after 1949 was strictly controlled by the central government, and all the universities were restructured according to the Soviet model, which viewed higher education as a means of serving the economic development of society. The aims of higher education that were laid down in the first national conference in 1950 were to train workers to grasp modern scientific and technological knowledge and to serve the people wholeheartedly by integrating the theories with practices. The majority of universities at that time were directly established and administered by different central ministries in order to train professional manpower for specific industries. It was believed that such a state-control model could best serve the centrally planned manpower needs.

The disciplines of the university were adjusted by the central government according to the local industrial development plan to improve the uneven geographical distribution of industry and university. A newly established Ministry of Education directly administered 14 comprehensive universities of which there was only one or two in each major region. The basic arts and science departments of all the old higher education institutions were amalgamated in these comprehensive universities to produce strong departments able to take the lead in advancing these disciplines. The Ministry of Education also administered six major normal universities that had departments of education and fine arts in addition to basic arts and science departments, and were responsible for higher teacher training in China's six major administrative regions. Another 25 normal universities were administered by provincial higher education bureaus and intended to lead teacher-training efforts for each province. Of the 38 engineering universities, about ten of the most distinguished polytechnic ones were administered by the Ministry of Education, while the rest belonged to other central ministries such as metallurgy and machine building. The 26 agricultural institutions and 29 medical institutions were administered by the respective central ministries and directly geared to national and provincial level development plans. Four institutes of political science and law under the Ministry of Justice trained legal–political cadres for broad regional needs. Six institutes of finance and economics under the Ministry of Finance served the six administrative regions. In addition, there was a small number of foreign language, fine arts and physical education institutes.

Since the Chinese Communist Party was developed and rooted in the rural, they had no experience in planning an urban university. Therefore the planning of the university in the urban environment largely followed the Soviet model. The universities were concentrated in the strictly zoned educational district on the urban fringe, performing as a 'green factory' cultivating intellectuals. The well-known university agglomeration, such as Yangpu District in Shanghai and Haidian District in Beijing, all came into being at that time. During the period of 1949–1957, most Chinese universities were reorganized according to the urban plan and were relocated to the urban fringe. The most representative case following the Soviet model was the development of eight universities in the academic zone of northwest Beijing. Along with the establishment of the eight universities, the city of Beijing expanded greatly toward the north. An urban road named Academic Road was constructed across the academic zone, along which the eight universities were aligned from south to north. All the universities had similar rectangle forms, similar area and similar campus borders. The space of the universities highlighted uniformity and coherency and reflected the supremacy of the socialist state power over society.

At the same time, the planning principles emphasizing the transition from a consumptive city to a productive city required all the state-owned enterprises and institutions to be self-sufficient units and to be responsible for the daily lives of their workers. That is to say, each unit was a micro society providing services in various aspects. A self-sufficient unit was also regarded as a planning measure to reduce traffic burdens and increase working efficiency. This phenomenon was particularly prominent in the universities that had to keep the image of an ivory tower. Universities remained self-sufficient and kept distance away from the society, producing the only social product, i.e. intellectuals, that had already been regulated by the national distribution regime. Staff housing and auxiliary facilities such as markets, shops and hospitals were all basic components in self-sufficient universities, which continued to exist until the 1990s and even until today. Guided by such a planning principle, different functional areas in the city had similar urban fabric. Taking Beijing Iron and Steel Institute and Beijing Textile Factory as an example, a similar grid road system divided the compounds into similar rectangle blocks; public buildings were arranged along the main axis and were distinct from the surrounding homogeneous teaching or producing buildings. The university and the factory showed nearly the same spatial forms.

Universities after 1978 opening up

From 1949 to 1978, the higher education system in China had undergone dramatic changes. It included the nationalization of the private universities and the adoption of the Soviet model in the early 1950s, the Great Leap Forward and the academic revolution from 1958 to 1960, the restructuring of the higher education system from 1961 to 1963, and the gradual improvement of university competitiveness from 1963 to 1965. Moreover, it also included the unprecedented destruction and serious shrinking of the higher education system during the so-called Cultural Revolution from 1966 to 1976 and the corresponding recovery from 1976 to 1978. It was important to note that the overall institutional framework of the Chinese higher education system as of 1979 was still characterized by the central planning model that had been adopted from the Soviets in the early 1950s. However, it could no longer fit the new requirement of fast socio-economic development in China. Dramatic changes have to be undertaken in the higher education sector. This was the domestic background to understand the contemporary Chinese higher education reform started in the early 1980s.

Socio-economic transformation in China beginning in the 1980s came along with the rapid advancements in science and technology, especially the revolutionary development of information and communication technology, which led the world into a new age of the knowledge-based society. As knowledge-based institutions, universities were called on to play a central role in socio-economic development. Furthermore, the knowledge-based economy is international by nature. Capital, production, management, market, labour, information, and technology were all organized across the national borders, which resulted in a strong tendency towards globalization. The exchanging of students and faculty members, the joint teaching and research programs and academic interaction especially over the internet formed an on-going and irreversible internationalizing trend in higher education and performed as the external driving forces for China's higher education reform.

The Chinese higher education system was characterized by a series of reforms from the 1980s up to the beginning of the twenty-first century. The universities were endowed with both autonomy and the legal status as enterprises in 1992. In 1993, according to the policies of educational industrialization, higher education was designated into the tertiary sector, which completely eliminated the nature of the universities as political institutions and mitigated their subordination to government decisions. Homogeneity and uniformity in the planned economy were replaced by heterogeneity and diversity, which was reflected not only in the organization of a single university but also in the whole higher education system. Various measures were taken in higher education reform, such as university merger, central–local joint development, public–private cooperation, non-state colleges, university towns and off-site campuses.

Local governments got more authority in decision-making through reform and they can establish their own universities according to the local economic and social development plans. For example, Ningbo University in Zhejiang Province was developed according to the urban strategy of a harbour city. It not only took into consideration the urban industrial structure in its educational tasks and curriculum design, but also located in the particular area between Ningbo City, Beilun Harbor, and Zhenhai District to accelerate the urbanization process. The state and non-state funding all flew into the university on the occasion of the new campus setting up and expansion. It enabled the universities to be an attractive pole in urban and regional development. The value of the university was largely considered to be in its combination of education and research with public service. Therefore the industrial clusters emerged around the university to search technological and intellectual support; service facilities such as restaurants and shops concentrated there as well. The university began to assume the role of an urban institution, extending its influence into the city and at the same time influenced by the city.

The emphasis on the service missions of the university led to a development coalition between the local government, enterprises and universities. Local government expected to accelerate GDP growth and urbanization process through university planning, enterprises tried to get much more profit through joint research and technology transfer, and the universities aimed to achieve a great leap forward by virtue of all kinds of opportunities. The coalition between local government, enterprises and universities made it possible for the various sectors to undertake the complex tasks through joint effort. However, it also induced the kind of profit-centred and project-oriented planning that was often blamed for selfishness and unsustainability. In February 2006, the Ministry of Education of China explicitly opposed the industrialization of higher education and proposed to make university spatial planning in an economic way and with a long-term view. The development of university towns was strictly audited by central government. All these efforts have demonstrated that the Chinese universities began to think carefully about its relations with the market and the enterprises, the boundary with the government and the political regime, and the ideal of free knowledge production.

Review on the evolution of the universities

Chinese universities have combined different missions and incorporated various even opposing forces throughout the long history of evolution. They keep on devising new combinatory models and strategies, changing the inner culture, and renovating the external mission. Some spatial forms emerged from time to time and were predominant in different historical periods, such as the combination of ritual orders with natural landscape by imperial bureaucracy, Western missionaries, conservative modernizers, and

Nationalist government. But the social values beneath similar spatial forms differentiated a lot from each other. For example, the original introduction of ritual orders into the picturesque space of university in ancient China was a simultaneous process along with the officialization of scholarly institutions, which was aimed to harness intellectuals for imperial civil service. In the Western missionary universities, however, the revival of the indigenous tradition was a measure to make them better situated in Chinese culture so as to reduce resistance in protesting Western interests. For the conservative modernizers, although they turned to Western universities for science and technology (S&T), they were not able to and would not like to revolutionize the imperial educational system, therefore they kept the traditional scholarly institutions as a reminiscence of past imperial privilege. Instead, the Nationalist government rejected thoroughly the feudal and imperial ideology, but the spatial organization of traditional scholarly institutions characterized by hierarchy and order met their requirement in consolidating one-party dictatorship.

Sometimes, even though the universities were embedded with the same social values, their spatial outcomes may also be different. Comparing the universities with nationalist spirits, Soviet influence and those after opening up, all of them were mobilized for economic development and national prosperity. But the Nationalist government promoted indigenous renewal, accentuating order and hierarchy in spatial organization; the soviet model performed as self-sufficient working unit concentrating various functions altogether and followed a strictly zoning approach; the universities after opening up, however, have built extensive networks with academic and non-academic institutions both internationally and domestically: spatial commercialization and differentiation has become its typical characteristics. It indicates that the space of university is influenced by multiple factors in society rather than the product of a sole object.

Looking through the development process, it is perceived that when there is consolidated national control and political power, the space of university tends to be harnessed by the gerontocratic for particular social uses, such as for civil service and economic growth. When the central dominance is loosened or preferably there is no official bureaucracy, diversified university spatial patterns will appear, as happened in China when universities were in search of modernity. As the world enters the global era and knowledge becomes an important means of social production, there is a convergence that universities across the world are increasingly involved in social development and they are more connected with and influenced by other social actors, including those out of their geographical boundaries. The secret of the enduring vitality of the university is that it never stops to find new ways of reinventing itself. Just as in history where there were a range of possibilities, the university now stands at the gateway of a range of futures, which are being shaped by a number of trends and emergent issues. To make a productive turn in the future, it is necessary to be aware of the situation, to understand the mechanism, and to grasp what is behind it.

References

Chen, X. (2008). *The Evolution of Chinese University Campus Morphology*. (PhD), Tongji University, Shanghai.

Hayhoe, R. (1987). Catholics and Socialists: The Paradox of French Educational Interaction with China. In R. Hayhoe & M. Bastid (Eds.), *China's Education and the Industrialized World*. Armonk and London: Sharpe.

Hayhoe, R. (1989). China's universities and Western academic models. *Higher Education, 18*(1), 49–85.

Huang, M., Shi, Y., & Zhang, Y. (1984). *Historical Materials on Shanghai University*. Shanghai: Fudan University Press.

Min, W. (2004). Chinese Higher Education: The Legacy of the Past and the Context of the Future. In P. G. Altback & T. Umakoshi (Eds.), *Asian Universities: Historical Perspectives and Contemporary Challenges*. Baltimore: The Johns Hopkins University Press.

Ministry of Education of China. (1947). *Educational Legislation*. Shanghai: Zhonghua Book Company.

Miyazaki, I. (1971). *China's Examination Hell: The Civil Service Examinations of Imperial China*. New York and Tokyo: Weatherhill.

Tsang, M. C. (2000). Education and national development in China since 1949: Oscillating policies and enduring dilemmas. *Economics of Education Review*, 579–618.

Wang, B., Guo, Q., Liu, D., He, X., Gao, Q., & Shi, K. (2007). *Introduction to the History of Chinese Education*. Beijing: Beijing Normal University Press.

Zhou, Y. (2007). *Modern Educational History in China*. Fuzhou: Fujian Education Press.

2 The role of universities in the knowledge society

Socio-spatial perspectives

There is no 'natural' way of talking about the space of the university since it is closely related with the social environment. With the arrival of the knowledge society, the university has become a strategic actor to promote social progress. To better understand the social attributes of the space of university, this chapter provides a socio-spatial review on the role of the university in the knowledge society. It focuses on the nature of space as a material product of society (the concrete aspect), the manifestation of social relations (the abstract aspect) and a means of social production (the instrumental aspect) (Lefebvre, 1991).

In the following, this chapter will first explain the characteristics of knowledge production in the knowledge society and the related spatial requirements on the university; then it will explore the relations between the university and other key actors, especially the interaction between the university, government and industry, in the process of university spatial development; finally it will discuss the engagement activities of the university in local development and their spatial manifestations.

University as knowledge infrastructure in the knowledge society

Space is a social product. It does not exist in itself; it is never primordially given or permanently fixed. Every society, more precisely every mode of production with its sub-variants, produces a space, its own space (Lefebvre, 1991). The concept of spatiality is itself imbued with a transformative dynamic: spatiality exists ontologically as a product of a transformation process, and always remains open to further transformation in the contexts of material life (Soja, 1989). Hence there is no 'natural' way to conceptualize space because it is produced in the context of social action (Harvey, 1989). Social structure remains the primacy in explaining spatial forms. Theories about space are generally deployment and specification of theories about social structure, which account for the characteristics of the particular social form, space, and of its articulation with other historically given forces and processes (Castells, 1977).

Understanding the space of university in contemporary times cannot be separated from the knowledge society. Over the past few decades, there have been a number of scholars arguing the change of the world economy. Although they used differentiated terms to illustrate this process, such as the learning economy (Johnson & Lundvall, 1994; Lundvall, 1996), the knowledge economy (Drucker, 1993; Nonaka, 1991; Powell & Snellman, 2004), the global economy (Dunning & Lundan, 2008; Grossman & Helpman, 1991) and the world economy (Sassen, 1994), there is one thing in common; that is, knowledge has become the driving force of economic development. Advanced services, such as finance, consulting, design and scientific innovation, which are at the core of the global economic processes, all can be reduced to knowledge generation and information flows; modes of organization of production in apparently low-tech sectors, have also been transformed, or are in the course of transformation, with the new use of knowledge bases (Castells, 2000). Knowledge is now fast becoming the basic means of production, sidelining capital, natural resources, and labour. The central wealth-creating activities are now being shifted from the allocation of capital and labour for productive uses to 'productivity' and 'innovation' through applications of knowledge (Drucker, 1993).

Nowadays, knowledge production is not the same as the traditional manner in which certain universities preserved their hierarchical position at the top of the 'knowledge pyramid'. Johnson and Lundvall's distinction of different kinds of knowledge may lead us to an initiative understanding of the production of knowledge. They propose a taxonomy including four kinds of knowledge: know-what, know-why, know-how, know-who (Johnson & Lundvall, 1994). Know-what refers to knowledge about facts and information, which can be broken into bits. Know-why refers to knowledge about principles and laws of motion in nature, in the human and in society. Know-what and know-why can be obtained through formal learning in the schools and universities in the normal channel, and can more easily be codified and transferred as information, some of which may even be sold in the market. Know-how refers to the skills and the capability to do something. It is basically tacit knowledge through practical experience, through learning-by-doing and through interacting with other experts active in the same field. Know-who involves information about who knows what and who knows to do what. It is rooted in social interacting and depends on the social capability to establish relationships with specialized groups in order to draw upon their expertise.

The production of knowledge embraces a social perspective on learning that focuses on the way people make sense of their experiences at work (Easterby-Smith, Araujo, & Burgoyne, 1999). The social perspective argues that learning is socially constructed and knowledge emerges from social interaction. The experiences people get through social interaction may derive from either explicit sources (codified scientific or engineering knowledge) or tacit sources (embodied in skilled personnel and/or technical routines). Explicit information involves a joint process of make sense of data and technical knowledge. It can be easily communicated and shared in product specifications or a scientific formula or a computer program. In contrast, tacit knowledge is highly personal, deeply rooted in action and in an individual's commitment to a specific context (Nonaka, 1991). It can be learned through situated practices, observation and emulation of skilled practitioners and socialization into a community of practice (Easterby-Smith et al., 1999).

The social interactive process in knowledge production goes beyond the particular business and management strategies of any individual firms and incorporates the cooperation and interaction among multiple knowledge producers and users. Innovation no longer proceeds sequentially from research to marketing. It is not a linear pathway from university research to commercial innovation to an ever-expanding network of newly formed companies. Instead, it is an interactive process in which a wide array of institutions can play a multiple role. Universities are no longer the sole providers of knowledge; firms and organizations draw knowledge in a variety of sources and they are also encouraged to adopt new organizational and management systems that can support knowledge-based production by themselves (Lundvall, 2002). Traditional modes of organization in the university, characterized by rigid borders and isolation from society, are being challenged as well. Knowledge production is melding among various knowledge infrastructures. Their spaces are more closely linked with each other and are embedded with functions of the others. Universities have to reposition themselves as players within a multi-pole network of knowledge producers and users and to build networks with other actors to facilitate the flow of knowledge, ideas and learning.

University as the contesting space of social relations

The production of space is a social process. It is not the work of a moment for a society to generate and produce an appropriated social space in which it can achieve a form by means of self-presentation and self-representation (Lefebvre, 1991). This act of creation is in fact a process. In the process, there is a dual relationship between people and space (Gottdiener & Hutchison,

2010). On the one hand, human beings act according to social factors such as gender, class, race, age and status within and in reaction to a given space. On the other hand, people create and alter space to express their own needs and desires. In addition to being a product of social relations, space is also a manifestation of social relations, and hence a manifestation of control, of domination and of power. Space is fundamental in any form of communal life and in any exercise of power (Foucault, 1984). There is a politics of space because space is political (Lefebvre, 1979). The political economy and the role of culture should be paid the same, if not higher, emphasis in the production of space compared with technological factors. Spatial politics shifts the research perspective from space to the processes of its production, embraces the multiplicity of space that are socially produced and made productive in social practices, and focuses on the contradictory, conflictual and ultimately political character of the processes of the production of space (Stanek, 2011).

The space of university is nestled with the interests of many groups, such as students, academicians, companies, the neighbourhood, government and developers. They all have a stake, something to gain or lose as a result of any change in the space of university. The role of university to affect local development depends crucially on its ability to balance the multiple relationships established between the place in question and its stakeholders (Russo, Berg, & Lavanga, 2007). And there are even more subtle and complicated relationships between the stakeholders themselves, affected in various ways by actions, decisions, policies, practices or goals both in and beyond the process of university spatial development. The specific interests that different stakeholders have may be partially contrasting and they may be not static but changing over time. The university thus often finds itself in the middle of political controversy when its physical development programs begin.

To smooth the process of university spatial development, it is encouraged to build partnerships between the university and community organizations. The related planning process can proceed in four stages: 1) to propose a kind of partnership when it is not necessary for either party to do so; 2) to develop some level of trust and some set of procedures of mutual benefit so as to guarantee the proceeding and the sustainable development of the partnership; 3) the partners take actions to make use of the resources, mobilize the related actors and evaluate the outcomes to achieve certain goals; and 4) internal structural and institutional changes of the partners to adapt themselves to the partnership (Wiewel & Lieber, 1998).

Similarly, the model of a harmonious relationship between the university, industry and government for innovation is described as a Triple Helix, in which each institutional sphere maintains its special features and unique identity while also taking the role of the other (Etzkowitz, 2003). In the Triple Helix model, industry operates as the locus of production, government performs as the source of contractual relations that guarantee stable interaction and exchange, and the university works as a source of new knowledge and technology. When fulfilling a particular purpose in society, the university, industry and government are conceptualized as intertwined spirals in a Triple Helix with different relations to each other. A primary institution is one that fulfils a central purpose in society; other institutions depend on it to fulfil their missions. The institution that acts as the core force changes over time as one replaces the other as the driving force.

The Triple Helix denotes a transformation in the relationship between the university, government and industry as well as within each of these spheres. As the institutions increasingly take the role of the other, the traditional match of institution to function is superseded. The Triple Helix model of simultaneously competing and cooperating institutional spheres differs from the situations in which the state encompasses industry and the university, for example, in the former Soviet Union, pre-reform China, and some European and Latin American countries. It is also different from the model of separate institutional spheres, for example, in the way that the US is supposed to operate, at least in theory, according to the laissez-faire principles (Etzkowitz, 2003). Starting from either the statist model or the laissez-faire model, there is a movement toward a new global model of Triple Helix with the dynamic university–government–industry interaction. The university is elevated to an equivalent status as government and industry, in contrast to the previous institutional configurations in which government and industry have always been major institutions and the university occupied a secondary status.

University engagement in local development

Space is not only the product of social relations, but also a tool. Space is more than the solely passive locus of social relations, the milieu in which their combination takes on body, or the aggregate of the procedures employed in their removal. It has an active role in the existing mode of social production. Space is permeated with social relations: it is not only supported and produced by social relations, but is also producing social relations (Lefebvre, 1979). Space occurs as a tool of power operation rather than merely an object (Foucault, 1984). There is a close and direct linkage between time–space relations and the generation of power as well as the reproduction of class structure (Giddens, 1981; Harvey, 1989). Power, the transformative capacity of people to change the social and material world, is closely shaped by knowledge and space–time (Harvey, 1989). In reality, social space 'incorporates' social actions, the actions of both individual and collective. Society is transformed through the production of space; space is a means of social production.

The space of university incorporates the engagement activities of universities with respect to their roles as economic contributors, commodified knowledge producers, shapers of human capital, and institutional actors in networks (Boucher, Conway, & van der Meer, 2003). These roles refer specifically to the activities of the university in: 1) employing workers, paying wages and salaries, buying local services and products and attracting students to spend money in the local economy; 2) producing and commercializing knowledge through intellectual property rights and technology transfer, cultivating science parks and spin-off firms; 3) educating students, providing life-long learning and cultivating intellectuals for companies; 4) participating in urban governance and institutional structuring formally or informally through linkages and networks with other urban actors (Boucher et al., 2003). The first two aspects focus on the universities' direct economic contribution while the latter two include non-economic sociocultural factors.

In the economic dimension, university spatial development is manipulated for the emergence and maintenance of an academic capitalist 'regime'. By regime, it means that there lies: 1) systematic revision and creation of policies to make the university engagement activities possible, 2) functional change in the interconnections between the state, the higher education system and other sectors supporting them, 3) basic change in academic practices (Rhoades & Slaughter, 2004). Within such a regime, the university has increasingly become involved in the formation of firms and science parks, often on the basis of new technologies originating in academic research, and has gradually transformed from the type of research university to entrepreneurial university. It has led to the more active financial management strategies of university resources, which extend beyond its intellectual properties and penetrate real estate development and other market-oriented practices.

In the socio-cultural dimension, university spatial development helps to establish the broader quality of the place in which the university is located. In service and symbol, today's universities in the knowledge era are the contemporary equivalent of cathedral precincts in medieval life, palaces and civic centres in the Renaissance, and railroad stations and central business districts in the age of commerce and urbanization (Dober, 2000). University engagement moves away from previous approaches driven largely by a 'deficit model', in which urban communities were viewed merely as possessing needs, and universities were seen as the expert to meet those needs (Altman, 2006). Today universities also play the roles of facilitator and action partner besides the role of technical resource provider (Mullins,

1996). When taking on the role of facilitator, universities are called on, largely because of their perceived position as an unbiased and independent party, to facilitate the projects that are affected by internal conflicts and political struggles among different community partners. When serving as action partner, universities contribute resources and finances to projects such as the development of non-profit corporations, affordable housing, community schools and health centres.

University engagement is largely considered as the third distinct role that the universities can play in serving society beyond merely teaching and research (Berger & Duguet, 1982; Boyer, 1990). The third mission is strongly related to the teaching and research activities of the universities, but goes beyond them. It penetrates into the organizational structure and institutional arrangement of the universities and has transformed the focus, content and evaluation of the teaching and research activities, bringing about new incentives and rewards. University engagement has great influence both on the out-reach activities and the in-reach activities of the university and tells something about how the university capabilities can be integrated into the economy and into society (Observatory of the European University, 2006).

References

Altman, J. H. (2006). *Matching University Resources to Community Needs: Case Studies of University–community Partnerships*. (PhD), Rutgers, The State University of New Jersey, New Brunswick.

Berger, G., & Duguet, P. (1982). *The University and the Community: The Problems of Changing Relationships*. Washington, DC: OECD Publications and Information Center.

Boucher, G., Conway, C., & van der Meer, E. (2003). Tiers of engagement by universities in their region's development. *Regional Studies, 37*(9), 887–897.

Boyer, E. (1990). *Scholarship Reconsidered: Priorities of the Professoriate*. Retrieved from http://www.hadinur.com/paper/BoyerScholarshipReconsidered.pdf.

Castells, M. (1977). *The Urban Question: A Marxist Approach*. Cambridge, MA: MIT Press.

Castells, M. (2000). *The Rise of the Network Society*. Malden, MA: Blackwell.

Dober, R. P. (2000). *Campus Landscape: Functions, Forms, Features*. Hoboken: John Wiley & Sons.

Drucker, P. (1993). *Post-Capitalist Society*. New York: Harper Business.

Dunning, J. H., & Lundan, S. M. (2008). *Multinational Enterprises and the Global Economy*. Cheltenham: Edward Elgar.

Easterby-Smith, M., Araujo, L., & Burgoyne, J. G. (1999). *Organizational Learning and Learning Organization: Developments in Theory and Practice*. London: Sage.

Etzkowitz, H. (2003). Innovation in innovation: The Triple Helix of university–industry–government relations. *Social Science Information, 42*(3), 293–337.

Foucault, M. (1984). Space, Knowledge, and Power. In P. Rabinow (Ed.), *The Foucault Reader*. New York: Pantheon.

Giddens, A. (1981). Time–Space Distanciation and the Generation of Power. In *A Contemporary Critique of Historical Materialism: Power, Property and the State*. London: Macmillan.

Gottdiener, M., & Hutchison, R. (2010). *The New Urban Sociology* (4th Edition). Boulder, CO: Westview Press.

Grossman, G. M., & Helpman, E. (1991). *Innovation and Growth in the Global Economy*. Cambridge, MA: MIT Press.

Harvey, D. (1989). *The Condition of Postmodernity: An Enquiry Into the Origins of Cultural Change*. Malden, MA: Blackwell.

Johnson, B., & Lundvall, B. Å. (1994). The learning economy. *Journal of Industry Studies, 1*(2), 23–42.

Lefebvre, H. (1979). Space: Social Product and Use Value. In J. W. Freiburg (Ed.), *Critical Sociology: European Perspectives*. New York: Irvington Publishers.

Lefebvre, H. (1991). *The Production of Space* (D. Nicholsonsmith, Trans.). Oxford and Cambridge: Blackwell Publishers.

Lundvall, B. Å. (1996). The Social Dimension of The Learning Economy. *Druid Working Papers*.

Lundvall, B. Å. (2002). The University in the Learning Economy. *Druid Working Papers*.

Mullins, R. L. (1996). *Town and Gown Partnerships for Renewing America's Neighborhoods*. (PhD), University of Louisville, Louisville, KY.

Nonaka, I. (1991). The knowledge-creating company. *Harvard Business Review, 69*(6), 96–104.

Observatory of the European University. (2006). *Strategic Management of University Research Activities: Methodological Guide*.

Powell, W. W., & Snellman, K. (2004). The knowledge economy. *Annual Review of Sociology, 30*(1), 199–220.

Rhoades, G., & Slaughter, S. (2004). Academic capitalism in the new economy: Challenges and choices. *American Academic, 1*(1), 37–59.

Russo, A. P., Berg, L. V. D., & Lavanga, M. (2007). Toward a sustainable relationship between city and university a stakeholdership approach. *Journal of Planning Education & Research, 27*(2), 199–216.

Sassen, S. (1994). *Cities in a World Economy*. London: Pine Forge Press.

Soja, E. W. (1989). *Postmodern Geographies: The Reassertion of Space in Critical Social Theory*. New York: Verso.

Stanek, L. (2011). *Henri Lefebvre on Space: Architecture, Urban Research, and the Production of Theory*. Minneapolis: University of Minnesota Press.

Wiewel, W., & Lieber, M. (1998). Goal achievement, relationship building, and incrementalism: The challenges of university-community partnerships. *Journal of Planning Education and Research, 17*(4), 291–301.

Part II

The global, national and local scales

3 Urban universities in the globalizing world

A wide range of scholars hold the opinion that today's world is transformed dramatically by globalization, which is strengthening the dominance of a world economy through capital control (Sassen, 1994; Wincott, 2002), challenging the governance of the nation-state with numerous international corporations and organizations (Bernstein & Cashore, 2007; Brenner, 1998), integrating the characteristic local traditions into a uniformed global culture (Cox, 1997; Porter, 2000). Dependence on the global network rather than the servicing of an environing region or a wider hinterland existed only for a few exceptional cities in the past, but now it has become the general rule for the majority of substantial cities anywhere (Taylor, 2004). The linkages binding a city have a direct and tangible effect on global affairs by all means.

In the global context of higher education, as perceived by Perry and Wiewel (2008), there is a transformation from the primacy of the American university mode to a more worldwide accession of universities in the increasingly important global cities. It was identified as the third academic revolution, which incorporates the 'multiversity' (Kerr, 2010) with much more mobility, more cross-national interaction and more global mechanisms. This chapter will analyze the changing global space of the universities and the interaction between the universities and the cities in the globalizing world by exploring the key factors of global urban competitiveness in the knowledge society, the urban strategies to promote global urban competitiveness, the requirements on and the responses of the universities, the changing geography of global university networks, and the strategic importance of global universities to global cities.

Assessing global urban competitiveness in the knowledge society

Within the global networks, cities are rarely equal. There is a sharply defined hierarchy of dominance within a tier of the most important world cities, and there is also a distinction of tiers (D. Smith & Timberlake, 2002). Cities may rise into the tier of world cities, they may drop from the order, and they may rise or fall in rank. Competition for dominance is always severe and the gap in global urban competitiveness between cities is inclined to be narrow. It was found that the global urban competitiveness of European and American cities hit an absolute decline (Ni & Kresl, 2012). For example, although New York still ranked first in global urban competitiveness in 2011–2012, its index fell by the largest. In contrast, the emerging economies are very active; the decline in their competitiveness is not significant, and some even continue to rise. For example, among the top ten fastest growing cities, i.e. San Jose (USA), Hong Kong (China), Suzhou (China), Changsha (China), Lagos (Nigeria), Georgetown (Guyana), Palo Alto (USA), Kingston (Jamaica), Xi'an (China), and Mannheim (Germany), most are from the emerging countries (Ni & Kresl, 2012).

The rise or decline of the cities in terms of global urban competitiveness has much to do with their functions (Ni & Kresl, 2012). Compared with the index in 2009–2010, the competitiveness index of technology centres in 2011–2012 improved dramatically while those of financial centres and manufacturing centres fell sharply. For example, San Jose, the core area of Silicon Valley, though suffering a lot from the global economy downturn and consumer environment recession, was still able to substantially enhance their competitiveness index as the fastest growing technology centre. New York and Houston suffered big losses in the financial crisis storm, and both ranked the top two largest dropping financial centres; Tokyo and London as the world's famous financial centre were also doomed to decline in the top five. The traditional manufacturing centres of developed countries in Europe and the United States were dropping significantly and the impact of the economic downturn on the manufacturing centres in developed countries was much more severe than in developing countries.

Global urban competitiveness comprises a variety of indices, representing the advantage of the cities in various aspects, some of which may have great disparity from each other. For example, Shanghai ranked No. 36 in 2011–2012 in terms of comprehensive global urban competitiveness, but a detailed examination revealed that while indices of internal and external connection, economic scale, industrial chain and elemental environment ranked ahead of the comprehensive index, those indices on patent application, development level, economic aggregation and public institution ranked relatively behind (Ni & Kresl, 2008, 2010, 2012). In particular, public institution ranked beyond the world top 500. It showed that while the economic structure and territorial endowment of Shanghai has risen to a higher level, human resources and the institutional milieu of Shanghai were still at the bottom of the ranking.

In a service- and knowledge-based society, human resource and institutional milieu parameters are more important than territorial endowment and economic structure for urban competitiveness (Webster & Muller, 2000). Human resources determine the extent to which activities in the cities can move up the value chains, while the institutional milieu and the quality of the place exert great influence on the return of human resources (Webster & Muller, 2000). Both human resources and institutional quality are grouped as intangible capital in wealth estimates made by the World Bank. An examination of the interrelations between the types of wealth and the income classes showed that intangible capital is the preponderant form of wealth worldwide and it was found that the share of produced capital in total wealth is virtually constant across all income groups, the share of natural capital in total wealth tends to fall with income, and the share of intangible capital rises (World Bank, 2006). The latter point makes perfect sense: rich counties and cities are rich largely because of the skills of their populations and the quality of the institutions supporting their economic activities.

Learning as the strategy of promoting urban competitiveness

As the formation of human capital and institutional context differs from one city to another, there is no single model about competitive cities. What successful cities have in common is their ability to mobilize and harness knowledge and ideas. Such ability may encompass the development of the educational and research infrastructures, a mechanism of coordinating the supply and demand of skilled individuals and a framework of organizational learning (Rutten, Boekema, & Kuijpers, 2003). This poses the requirement for the cities to become learning cities or learning regions so as to be competitive in the global economy (Florida, 1995). Learning cities function as a collector and repository of knowledge and ideas and provide the underlying environment or infrastructures that facilitate the flow of knowledge and ideas.

The notion of learning not only focuses on what our society is becoming, but also underlines how we should and can act in response to new situations. It reintroduces a critical dimension, allowing the cities to face the possibility of assimilating the incredible amount of new knowledge that they regularly produce and of making full use of the networked relations that are dominant in society. Learning is the chief means by which cities can become more vibrant, healthier, safer, more inclusive and more sustainable. However, learning is largely intangible and it cannot be arranged by order. What is important therefore is to concentrate on the conditions that favour the emergence of the process of learning since they constitute the only factor that is in our power to affect. As an important means to promote learning, technological progress facilitates the frequent exchange among cities and individuals and is helpful to the flow of knowledge. Institutional efforts also make a contribution by encouraging the setting up of lifelong learning systems and the development of learning communities.

A watershed in global thinking about learning appeared in the European Year of Lifelong Learning in 1996. In that year both the OECD and UNESCO released their major reports on lifelong learning, and a number of European nations launched the learning city and regional initiatives. The reports of the OECD and UNESCO illuminated the importance of community-based learning and the understanding that learning is embedded in everyday community settings, such as the family, the neighbourhood, the school and the workplace. Such a concern of learning illustrates a paradigm shift: learning can no longer be confined to a settled space–time, but may develop across multiple places and over a lifetime. The 'learning' model has spread far beyond the world of education and into every cranny of economic and social life. It is now increasingly accepted that any organization, profit-making or not, needs to strengthen its educational and 'learning' side. Learning as a phenomenon may generalize at all levels of our society and may offer a model for organizing the space, time, work and lives of our society.

In the first years of the development of learning cities, most nations appear to have focused on practical issues of learning how to build a process or structural model relevant to their community. Later, there has been rapidly increasing interest in investigating the differences a learning city can make at both the macro and the micro levels (Faris, 2006). For example, the United Kingdom government has supported several seminal guides, reports and initiatives to assess the processes and outcomes of promoting the learning community. 'A Guide to Assessing Practice and Progress: Learning Communities' was field-tested in 1998–1999, followed by an analytical survey of learning cities in 2000, and then by a learning community test-bed initiative in 28 sites. In Australia, the launch of the Victorian State Learning Towns Program in 2000 was followed a year later by a state-wide evaluation. Evaluation tools and reports have also been developed at the local level in Hume city and Mt Evelyn, for instance.

Given the many attempts in various countries, transformation into learning cities is only possible if the transformative learning of individuals and groups is systematically fostered. Social learning groups may range from those on the smallest scale (learning circles), through to those on the largest or global scale (virtual global learning communities). The degree to which the organizations within each sector become learning organizations through investing in the learning of all their members and strategically leveraging the organizations' human and social capital is one factor deciding the transformative power of a learning city. A new paradigm that focuses on suffusing learning strategies in the policy, planning and programs of the civic, economic, educational, public and voluntary sectors increases the probability of achieving sustainable economic, environmental and social development (Faris, 2006).

Diversified organization of universities for learning cities

In the knowledge-based society, there are knowledge infrastructures that provide knowledge workers and facilitate life-long learning. Infrastructure is distinguished from other components of the capital stock and from other widely used inputs primarily because of their attributes of indivisibility, multi-user and generic (K. Smith, 2005). Knowledge infrastructures possess the technical and economic characteristics that are similar to those of physical infrastructure such as roads, harbours, electricity production and distribution systems, and telecommunications networks. They are a complex of public and private organizations and institutions whose role is the production, maintenance, distribution, management and protection of knowledge.

Universities are typical knowledge infrastructures in learning cities. They are destined to play a fundamental role in global cities given the requirement on learning in every corner of the city. And the role of universities in this aspect is likely to further increase. Consequently, a remarkably diverse array of organizations of universities – such as virtual universities, franchise universities, corporate universities, mobile universities and academic brokers – has emerged to create new opportunities to meet the growing social demand. They transcend the conceptual, institutional and geographical boundaries of traditional universities.

Virtual university

The elimination of the physical distance barrier as a result of the information and communication technology revolution makes it possible to provide higher education programs through electronic media, typically the internet. Virtual universities share a borderless nature that connects the universities and the participants in a network system. Virtual universities have been widely hailed as the future of distance higher education, due to their cost-effectiveness, economies of scale and the ability to reach a wide international clientele. However, there are also drawbacks of the virtual universities as compared to the traditional campus-based institutions, such as the lack of face-to-face contact between students and teachers, the erosion of traditional academic values, the loss of a sense of community and shared tradition, technological development at the expense of pedagogical standards, a tendency towards cultural homogenization and an emphasis on quantity over quality.

Franchise universities

In many parts of the world, predominantly in south and southeast Asia and the formerly socialist countries of eastern Europe, there has been a proliferation of overseas 'validated courses' offered by franchise institutions operating on behalf of British, American, Australian and other universities. The cost of attending these franchise institutions is much less, usually one-fourth to one-third of what it would cost to enrol in the mother institutions (World Bank, 2002). It was estimated that one-fifth of the 80,000 foreign students enrolled in Australian universities are studying at offshore campuses, mainly in Malaysia and Singapore (Bennell & Pearce, 1998). In China, franchise universities are still at the primary stage of development, but there is a growing trend.

Corporate universities

A corporate university is an educational entity and a strategic tool designed to assist its parent organization to achieve certain missions by conducting activities of cultivating both individual and organizational learning (Allen, 2002). It is a powerful rival to the traditional universities in the area of continuing education. Corporate universities are most commonly found in the United States, a nation that has more leading corporations than any other. In 1993, there were only 400 companies owning corporate universities in the United States. By 2001, this number had increased to 2,000 (Hearn, 2001). Corporate universities may operate through their own networks of physical campuses (examples are Disney, Toyota, and Motorola), as virtual universities (e.g. IBM and Dow Chemical), or through an alliance with existing tertiary education institutions (as do Bell Atlantic, United HealthCare, and United Technologies) (UNESCO, 2005). Some corporate universities have already been accredited formally to grant college degrees, such as McDonald's, Bell Telephone and the Ford Motor Company.

Mobile universities

With the cross-border flows of knowledge and ideas, more and more students and scholars are being assimilated into international organizations and are losing their university identities or national characters. Knowledge is expanding and diversifying rapidly through networks around international symposia and specialized research journals. The development of 'summer universities' operating at the frontier between research and teaching enables the researchers to disseminate new knowledge more efficiently and rapidly even than through traditional symposia and congresses. These activities show strong features of 'de-territorialization': the events organized by these networks are deserting the university campuses for large hotels; scholars meet regularly at itinerant congresses and seminars; the funding of the meetings becomes increasingly independent of the academic institutions, and is covered for the most part by the extra-academic institutions or participants themselves.

Academic brokers

There are also some virtual, often web-based, entrepreneurs specialized in bringing together the suppliers and consumers of educational services in many different areas, such as Connect Education Inc. and Electric University Network that provide brokering services and virtual counselling. A growing virtual real estate market, which builds, leases, and manages virtual campuses, is also emerging (Abeles, 1998). For example, IBM and others are working with traditional physical campuses to create 'Thinkpad U' where all the students and faculty are equipped with portable computers and the campus is wired to the internet. Multimedia educational software is produced to serve the training needs of educational clients as well. Dozens of web-based companies act as clearinghouses between the schools and prospective students, offering information about academic and financial resources.

The changing global geography of urban universities

The diversified and flexible modes in the organization of university, coupled with the frequent interaction and complex networks between the universities and cities, have transformed the global geography of urban universities. The space of universities is flowing across urban and national boundaries as promoted by the cross-border mobility and setting up of branch campuses. There is no longer a simple centrality in the global university system as dominated by those in developed countries in the past. Rather, it assumes several new geographical forms including international cooperation and alliances that incorporate universities in the countries at various development levels, as well as a grid of nodes of higher education and research activities caused by the strategic localization of global universities in global cities.

The flowing space

As the world economies become increasingly interconnected, the international skills needed to operate on a global scale have become increasingly important. Globally oriented firms seek internationally-competent workers who speak foreign languages and have the intercultural skills needed to successfully interact with international partners. Governments aim to improve academic standards and enhance the quality of education and research in light of those international standards now achieved in advanced countries. Individuals are looking for higher education to broaden their horizons and help them to better understand the world's languages, cultures and business methods. The growing demand for the international sharing of education and training, coupled with the borderless nature in the organization of knowledge and in the creation of intangible capital, has translated into a general trend towards the flowing space of global universities.

The proportion of international students in tertiary enrolments provides a good indication of the extent of mobility in higher education across the world. Over the past three decades, the number of students enrolled in tertiary education outside their countries of citizenship had risen from 0.8 million worldwide in 1975 to 3.3 million in 2008, a more than fourfold increase. Since 2000, the number of foreign tertiary students enrolled worldwide had increased by 70% until 2008, an average annual increase of nine percentage points (OECD, 2010). Growth in the internationalization of tertiary education has accelerated, mirroring the globalization of economies and societies. The United States, the United Kingdom, Germany, France and Australia received more than 50% of all the foreign students worldwide. Since 2005 the rate of growth in non-OECD destinations has been higher than in OECD member countries, which reflects the increasing preference to study in emerging countries. In absolute terms, the largest numbers of international students are from China and India, holding 17.1% (not including an additional 1.4% from Hong Kong, China) and 6.8% in the total OECD destinations respectively, and 15.7% and 5.7% in the total reported destinations around the world (OECD, 2010).

As the largest foreign student output country, the number of Chinese student studying abroad was up to 1.27 million at the end of 2010 (National Bureau of Statistics of China, 2011). Their destination of choice was first the United States, followed closely by Japan, with 21.6% and 15.3% respectively of all international Chinese students studying abroad (OECD, 2010). The enrolment of foreign students in China began in 1950, with 33 students from five countries in eastern Europe. In 2011, the number of foreign students in China had increased to nearly 300,000, from 194 countries and regions, in 660 Chinese higher education institutions (China Education Association for International Exchange, 2011). The top ten countries of origin were South

Korea, the United States, Japan, Thailand, Vietnam, Russia, Indonesia, India, Pakistan, Kazakhstan. Besides, France, Mongolia, Germany was also listed in the countries of origin, with over 5,000 students in China.

Meanwhile, universities are developing new sites, sometimes overseas, to build up new core markets and generate resources to cross-subsidize the less profitable but important campuses. For example, New York University has a host of foreign facilities used for study-abroad programs, referred to as Global Academic Centres. It operates 14 academic sites in Africa, Asia, Australia, Europe, the Middle East, North and South America as both degree-granting research university campuses and study-abroad sites. Global networks are absorbing the universities into a distributed global system. Universities seem increasingly aware that the costs of not developing global networks may be rising. These include losing market share to foreign organizations and declining intellectual capital.

As investigated by R. Becker (2009), the total number of international branch campuses worldwide grew from 35 in 1999 to 162 in 2009, including 78 branches operated by United States universities. In addition to the United States, the home countries of the institutions with international branches included Australia, the United Kingdom, France and India. As of 2009, the top host country for branch campuses was the United Arab Emirates, comprising 40 branch campuses, about one-fourth of the total. Other leading host countries include China, Singapore, Qatar and Canada. The United Arab Emirates has been able to attract more campuses than any other country, primarily because of its high student demand for tertiary education, a need to build a knowledge society and economy to reduce its dependence on the export of oil, attractive funding and support 'packages' (such as tax-free trade zones) for foreign institutions that establish a campus there and, more importantly, the United Arab Emirates government is considered stable and more 'pro-Western' than many others in the region.

An emerging key shift in the setting up of branch campuses is about who is setting up where. Traditionally, it is 'North to South', i.e. colleges and universities in developed nations creating campuses in the developing world. This model is still the most prevalent, describing 51% of the branch campuses (R. Becker, 2009). But as the slim majority suggests, other models are now reaching critical mass as well. 30% of the branch campuses are now considered 'North to North', with both home and host nations being the developed nations. Much of this kind of growth has taken place with branches in Singapore and Australia. 'South to South' branch campuses are also on the rise. In 2006 there were only five such examples, but in 2009 the number rose to 26, with source countries including Chile, Iran, Lebanon, Malaysia, Mexico, the Philippines and Sri Lanka, and the key host country being the United Arab Emirates.

The new centrality

Cross-border development of global universities does not mean that education and research activities are proceeding in a mere borderless space of flows. Rather, the centrality still exists in the global university system, but assumes different forms. On the one hand, international cooperation and university alliances are established to deal with the emerging issues that any single university cannot fulfil. On the other hand, cross-border development of global universities is developed strategically for particular interests, with global cities as the prior consideration in the choice of places, thus contributing to the concentration of global universities in global cities. The space of centrality works as an important counterpart to the space of flows in the global university networks.

Although developing global solidarity is undoubtedly more difficult than developing the national or regional practices of solidarity, it is nevertheless still possible. By building global networks to exchange information and provide material aid, universities in different parts of the world have in fact been successful in challenging the attempts of mobility to play them against each other. The much greater availability of information and the ease of communication resulting from innovations in computer technology have paradoxically facilitated increasing university contacts around the world. Frequent exchange among universities contributes to the formation of university alliances and international cooperation, which are modelled through pooling of resources and some coordinated budgeting.

For example, the Worldwide Universities Network, an invitation-only and non-profit group of 18 universities from Australia, Canada, China, New Zealand, Norway, South Africa, Brazil, the United Kingdom and the United States, was founded in 2000 to provide financial and infrastructural support to member universities to allow student and staff exchanges, the development of international training programs and collaborative research work. All the members have agreed to carry out research and training on a collaborative basis, principally by organizing online and interactive video seminars and by financing exchanges of research students and staff. It has also developed research-based degree programs as well as other online training courses that are provided jointly by academic staff from several of the participating universities.

Most distinctively, considering the many cross-border branch campuses that global universities have open to seek a broader educational market, the flowing space of global universities is not developed in a mere natural and borderless way. Rather, there is a tendency for the creation of transnational universities along the lines of transnational corporations. Such universities, operating to maximum benefit in outlets around the world, have taken advantage of their corporate organizational form. This enables them to internalize the international exploitation of their assets in the context of locational risks and opportunities generated by the differences in the regional forms of regulation and the gaps in international regulatory coordination. Competition between regional regulatory and institutional systems is happening, with transnational universities picking and choosing their preferred regulator. At this point, the historic alignment between the university and the city is giving way to one based more on global frameworks and corporate interests.

Thus the global universities are shifting activities between locations, sites and even cities to maximize their benefit, with profound consequences for their host cities. The university is looking for an attractive city to locate the new campus in order to attract more talents. At the same time, the city is also looking for competitive universities to promote its competence by virtue of university resources. Thus there is reciprocal attraction and mutual selection between the university and the city. Top universities seek top cities, and vice versa. Some cities have succeeded in attracting the universities, while some have failed. This has contributed to the concentration of global universities in global cities. For example, the development of international branch campuses, such as the 14 branch campuses of New York University as mentioned above, happened first in the top global cities such as London, Paris and Shanghai. The national wave of cross-city branch campus development in China in recent years has also shown a similar trend in terms of the strategic localization of key universities in key cities. All the home universities are listed in the Chinese '211' project, a national project to develop key research universities; and all the host cities are the fastest-growing cities, some of which are special economic zones enjoying favourable national policies.

Strategic importance of global universities in global cities

Global universities stand at the intersection of the knowledge economy and the network society. They are of strategic importance in the globalizing world. The global university networks have contributed to the broader access to higher education and promoted the accumulation of human capital for urban development. Over the past decades, universities across the world have experienced an explosive growth in student numbers, described by some as a 'massification' of higher education. Enrolments in higher education in the world almost doubled between the early 1970s and 1990, the estimated number of students rising from 28 to 69 million, and reaching a figure of 122 million in 2002 (UNESCO Institute for Statistics, 2005).

According to certain projections, the student population could reach 150 million in 2025 (Moe & Blodget, 2000). This trend is not confined to wealthy countries. In Africa, Asia and Latin America, strong population growth has helped to swell numbers at the primary and secondary levels, thereby boosting enrolments in higher education, although to a much lesser extent than in Europe or North America. Thus while enrolment ratios in the wealthy countries rose from 2.2% in the 1960s to 59% in 2002 in Europe and from 7.2% to 55% in North America, rates in the least developed countries barely increased from 1.3% to 4% (UNESCO Institute for Statistics, 2005). With a marked disparity between rich and poor countries, participation in higher education has increased dramatically in general.

The massification of higher education has enhanced the role of universities in cultivating human capital. Human capital is a means of production, into which additional investment yields additional output. Different from monetary capital that grows at a relatively higher or lower rate depending on the period of prosperity or the period of recession and depression, human capital has a uniformly rising rate of growth over a long period of time (G. S. Becker, 1993). That is to say, the current generation is qualitatively developed by the effective inputs of education, and the future generation is more benefited by the advanced research undertaken by the current generation (Hansen, 1970). This is the cumulative growth of human capital formation. In this sense, educational investment is more promising and profitable compared with the investment in other durable goods. Therefore, the problem of scarcity of tangible capital in the labour surplus cities can be resolved by accelerating the rate of human capital formation with both private and public investment in education sectors.

The rapid expansion of higher education has intensified the financial pressures on universities and led to a greater interest in recruiting foreign students whose tuition fees are often higher than for local students (UNESCO, 2005). Therefore, global universities are increasingly relying on revenues from the foreign markets. The long-term trend towards a greater internationalization of higher education is likely to have a growing impact on the local balance of payments in services as a result of the revenues from tuition fees and domestic consumption by international students. The global university networks, in the form of student mobility, cross-border electronic delivery of flexible educational programs, campuses abroad and transnational collaboration, generate an entry for the cities into the global circuits and are relevant to the trade dimension of international higher education services as well as other related interests. From a macroeconomic perspective, international negotiations on the liberalization of trade in services highlight the trade implications of the internationalization of education services (UNESCO, 2005).

The predictable emergence of global networks implies that the decentralized structures organized along network lines could be a valuable supplement to the permanent sources of funding and hierarchical organizational patterns. For the cities, this is a means of building a network of academic excellence rather than building a single world-class academic institution. For those cities and countries that have invested insufficiently in university-type institutions, they could and above all should think of investing in network organizations that anticipate the foreseeable development of academic institutions. This is all the more advisable since the economic costs of academic networks are much less than those involved in the creation of large university establishments (UNESCO, 2005). Networking enables the cities to establish a higher education system or to improve its quality without having to wait to secure large investments or to be in a position to make long-term commitments. It is easier for these cities to link up to the network structures that are themselves linked to other institutions or existing networks within the framework of regional or international cooperation.

Furthermore, the development of global university networks is more than a simple case of 'fitting in' to the existing environment of their hosting cities and countries. It is also in a way that is consistent with the university's strategy and operations in other places of the world. Local environment may have to be inventively moulded if the university organization and strategy in one city are not to become inconsistent with those in other cities. Hence, in China for example, when foreign universities first settled in, they altered particular strategies in terms of the admission criteria (taking the Chinese national college entrance examination as the reference), tuitions fees and expenses (much cheaper than in the mother institutions), course arrangement (including the language curriculum design), and the cultural and social expectations for employment (such as the role of the labour unions). But as more and more foreign universities move in, the educational environment in China is being transformed with the acceptance and appreciation of the standards and norms that are popular and dominant in other places in the world, such as granting universities a certain autonomy in deciding the admission criteria. Rather than being passive followers of urban strategies, global universities have often inventively transformed the local institutions and the urban development trajectory.

References

Abeles, T. P. (1998). The academy in a wired world. *Futures, 30*(7), 603–613.

Allen, M. (Ed.). (2002). *The Corporate University Handbook: Designing, Managing, and Growing a Successful Program*. New York: AMACOM.

Becker, G. S. (1993). *Human Capital: A Theoretical and Empirical Analysis* (3rd Edition). Chicago: The University of Chicago Press.

Becker, R. (2009). *International Branch Campuses: Markets and Strategies*. London: Observatory on Borderless Higher Education.

Bennell, P., & Pearce, T. (1998). The internationalisation of higher education: Exporting education to developing and transitional economies. *International Journal of Educational Development, 23*(2), 215–232.

Bernstein, S., & Cashore, B. (2007). Can non-state global governance be legitimate? An analytical framework. *Regulation & Governance, 1*(4), 347–371.

Brenner, N. (1998). Global cities, glocal states: Global city formation and state territorial restructuring in contemporary Europe. *Review of International Political Economy, 5*(1), 1–37.

China Education Association for International Exchange. (2011). *Statistics of Foreign Students in China 2011*.

Cox, K. R. (1997). *Spaces of Globalization: Reasserting the Power of the Local*. New York: Guilford Press.

Faris, R. (2006). *Learning Cities: Lessons Learned*. Retrieved from http://www.resdac.net/documentation/pdf/forum_aga/2012/en/Learning_Cities.pdf.

Florida, R. (1995). Toward the learning region. *Futures, 27*(5), 527–536.

Hansen, L. W. (1970). *Education, Income, and Human Capital*. National Bureau of Economic Research; distributed by Columbia University Press, New York.

Hearn, D. R. (2001). *Education in the Workplace: An Examination of Corporate University Models*. Retrieved from www.newfoundations.com/OrgTheory/Hearn721.html.

Kerr, C. (2010). *The Uses of the University* (5th Edition). Cambridge, MA: Harvard University Press.

Moe, M. T., & Blodget, H. (2000). *The Knowledge Web: People Power – Fuel for the New Economy Pot*. New York: Merrill Lynch.

National Bureau of Statistics of China. (2011). *Report No.13 on the Socio-Economic Achievement of 11th Five-Year Plan: Significant Achievement of Educational Development*.

Ni, P., & Kresl, P. K. (2008). *Global Urban Competitiveness Report 2007–2008*. Beijing: Social Sciences Academic Press.

Ni, P., & Kresl, P. K. (2010). *Global Urban Competitiveness Report 2009–2010*. Beijing: Social Sciences Academic Press.

Ni, P., & Kresl, P. K. (2012). *Global Urban Competitiveness Report 2011–2012*. Beijing: Social Sciences Academic Press.

OECD. (2010). *Education at a Glance 2010: OECD Indicators*. Retrieved from http://dx.doi.org/10.1787/eag-2015-en.

Perry, D., & Wiewel, W. (2008). The University, the City, and Land: Context and Introduction. In W. Wiewel & D. C. Perry (Eds.), *Global Universities and Urban Development: Case Studies and Analysis*. Armonk: M. E. Sharpe.

Porter, M. E. (2000). Location, competition, and economic development: Local clusters in a global economy. *Economic Development Quarterly, 14*(1), 15–34.

Rutten, R., Boekema, F., & Kuijpers, E. (2003). Economic Geography of Higher Education: Setting the Stage. In R. Rutten, F. Boekema, & E. Kuijpers (Eds.), *Economic Geography of Higher Education: Knowledge Infrastructure and Learning Regions*. New York: Routledge.

Sassen, S. (1994). *Cities in a World Economy*. London: Pine Forge Press.

Smith, D., & Timberlake, M. (2002). Hierarchies of Dominance among World Cities: A Network Approach. In S. Sassen (Ed.), *Global Networks, Linked Cities*. New York: Routledge.

Smith, K. (2005). Economic Infrastructures and Innovation Systems. In C. Edquist (Ed.), *Systems of Innovation: Technologies, Institutions and Organizations*. Oxon: Routledge.

Taylor, P. J. (2004). *World City Network: A Global Urban Analyses*. New York: Routledge.

UNESCO. (2005). *Towards Knowledge Societies*. Retrieved from http://unesdoc. unesco.org/images/0014/001418/141843e.pdf.

UNESCO Institute for Statistics. (2005). *UIS Education Database*. Retrieved from http://data.uis.unesco.org/Index.aspx?DataSetCode=EDULIT_DS&popupcusto mise=true&lang=en.

Webster, D., & Muller, L. (2000). *Urban Competitiveness Assessment in Developing Country Urban Regions: The Road Forward*. Retrieved from http://www.ucl. ac.uk/dpu-projects/drivers_urb_change/urb_economy/pdf_urban_dev_finance/ WorldBank_Webster_Urban%20Co.pdf.

Wincott, D. (2002). *Global Capital, Political Institutions, and Policy Change in Developed Welfare States*. Cambridge: Cambridge University Press.

World Bank. (2002). *Constructing Knowledge Societies: New Challenges for Tertiary Education*. Retrieved from http://siteresources.worldbank.org/TERTIARY EDUCATION/Resources/Documents/Constructing-Knowledge-Societies/Con structingKnowledgeSocieties.pdf.

World Bank. (2006). *Where Is the Wealth of Nations? Measuring Capital for the 21st Century*. Retrieved from http://siteresources.worldbank.org/INTEEI/214578-1110886258964/20748034/All.pdf.

4 University–city coalitions between the state and the market in China

One of the major impacts of globalization is related to the fundamental change in the philosophy of governance and the way that the public sector is managed (Flynn, 1997; Hood, 1991). The shift from 'government' to 'governance' has been widely debated (Kooiman, 1993; Peters & Pierre, 1998; Rhodes, 1997; Rosenau & Czempiel, 1992). Inherited geographies of the state power were fundamentally rescaled through the relationships on the supranational (transnational) and subnational (cities or regions) levels (Brenner, 2004). Since the economic reforms, the Chinese state apparatus has abandoned the direct allocation of production materials, capital, land and workforce while consolidating its regulatory power at the local level along with the decentralization of economic power and authority. Cities get more power of decision making and become the strategic arenas of state governance. The broader economic reforms after the later 1970s in China have also led to the conscious retreat of the state from being the sole provider of social services (Hawkins, 2000; Mok, 1997, 2000). Governments are conceived as 'facilitators' instead of 'service providers'. Both state and non-state actors are involved in the funding, regulation and provision/delivery of higher education. The orientation of teaching, research and service activities at the universities is being transformed, and so is the relation between the universities and the cities.

This chapter will analyze the spatial practices of the universities and the cities and their corresponding interactions in the process of China's reform, which was characterized by a series of measures redefining the relationships between the state and the market. It will discuss the changing state governance in the Chinese market-oriented reform, the influences on urban development strategies and the higher education system, the role of universities for national and regional innovation, the changing university–city relations and the underpinning values.

The devolved state power in China through market-oriented reform

Chinese economic reforms, taking advantage of market principles, began in 1978 and were carried out in two stages. The first stage, in the late 1970s and early 1980s, involved the decollectivization of agriculture, the opening up of the country to foreign investment, and the permission for entrepreneurs to start up businesses. However, most industry remained state-owned. The second stage of reform, in the late 1980s and 1990s, involved the privatization and contracting out of state-owned industry and the lifting of price controls, protectionist policies and regulations, although state monopolies in sectors such as banking and petroleum still remained. The private sector grew remarkably, accounting for over two-thirds of China's GDP by 2011, a figure larger in comparison with many Western countries (J. Yang, 2011). From 1979 to 2007, unprecedented growth occurred in China, with the national economy increasing annually by 9.8% on average (Liu & Zhou, 2008). China's economy became the second largest after the United States.

The Chinese reforms were accompanied by the so-called 'four modernizations' of agriculture, industry, science and technology, and defence. A new 'socialist market economy' was to replace the previous 'centrally planned economy'. The mode of governance associated with the classic ideal type of bureaucracy is in the process of being deconstructed. In its place are the emerging forms of governance that bring both state and non-state actors into the policy process, and transfer control to bodies operating either on the margins of the state or outside its boundaries altogether. Decentralization and marketization are perceived as the two major distinguishing features of Chinese reform (Morris, Hassard, & Sheehan, 2002). Decentralization shifted power from the central government to the regional and urban levels, while marketization introduced non-state actors into the provision of public services. All these measures were taken under the strict control of the Community Party of China and in a much more pragmatic and gradual process, based on trial and error, which resulted in a mixed transitional economy in China characterized by the co-existence of the new and old institutions.

Decentralization: rescaling state power from the central to the local

Fiscal reform is generally identified as a milestone in China's reform because it has redefined the financial responsibility of the central and local (provincial and municipal) governments, to allow the latter greater financial flexibility and legitimacy in managing local development (Jin, Qian, &

Weingast, 2005; Lin & Liu, 1998; Oi, 1992; Tong, 1989; Weingast, Qian, & Montinola, 1995; Wong, 1991; T. Zhang & Zou, 2001). The fiscal system in China was highly centralized before the reforms. It was consistent with China's centralized production and resource allocation system that had been adopted during the pre-reform era. In the centralized fiscal system, local governments relied on state budgetary allocation for capital investment in the maintenance and improvement of urban infrastructure. The cities were established, financed and managed by the central state as the functional nodes of the centrally planned economic system that were connected through vertical linkages (McGee, Lin, Marton, Wang, & Wu, 2007). There were, however, few incentives for local fiscal responsibility and effort. In addition, there was a lot of dissatisfaction in relation to excessive budgetary control over local services, the discouragement of local planning, and the disregard of regional differences by a uniform system.

With the objective to make the localities fiscally self-sufficient, to reduce the central state's own fiscal burden, and to provide incentives for local authorities to promote economic development, China has gone through several rounds of fiscal reforms in an effort to decentralize its fiscal system and fiscal management since the late 1970s (Central Committee of the Communist Party of China, 1993a, 2003; State Council of China, 1980, 1985, 1988). The decentralized fiscal arrangement enacted the revenue-sharing arrangements under the principle of dividing revenues and expenditures, with each level of government responsible for balancing its own budget. Although the state budgetary allocation of funds for local revenues was reduced, local governments were given greater autonomy in financing local development, particularly in the use of surplus revenues after the agreed quota of remittance to the central government was met. By introducing schemes that allowed both the central state and local governments to share above-target revenues, these reforms changed the zero-sum character in central–local relations in the central fiscal system, where one side only gained what the other lost (Tong, 1989). The structural changes in the fiscal system were designed to steer central–local relations towards a system of mutual benefits and shared risks, away from the subordination that had characterized central–local relations in the pre-reform era.

Marketization: reducing the role of the state in the public domain

Marketization, i.e. the development of market mechanisms and the adoption of market criteria within the public sector, is another major feature in Chinese reform. Before the reform, everyone in China belonged to a certain work unit. Once assigned work by the labour bureaus, workers enjoyed life tenure and generous perks given by the work units. Work units acted as the first level of the multi-tier hierarchy within the centrally-planned system. The state provided all kinds of social services through the work units and was responsible for full employment, income equalization, controlled pricing, social security, occupational benefits, health services, housing and all manners of subsidies. Private ownership was regarded as an evil. In contrast, collectivism was considered as superior to reduce disparities in living standards and consumption.

After the reform, much of the power of the work units was removed, although the term 'work unit' was still used in the context of state-owned enterprises and institutions. The new course was founded on a different interpretation of the socialist construction, and the key tasks were to resolve the conflicts between people's rising material aspirations and the backwardness of productive forces. Economic growth was put into first place while equality was considered secondary. It was explicitly agreed that it was good if a few got rich first. Private enterprises, particularly foreign direct investment, were greatly encouraged. As social services were considered not directly related to economic growth, the state set lower priority for investment and encouraged joint responsibility and diversification in the provision, funding and regulation of social welfare. In an effort to make state-owned enterprises more economically efficient and competitive, Chinese leaders took significant steps to open them up to a certain degree to market forces, with a view to more capitalist-style organizational forms and enabling them to be more market-responsive.

The reduction of the state's role in the public domain, therefore, can be viewed as a transfer of the social responsibility for production and financing from the state to non-state sectors, namely, the market, the family, the informal sector and individuals. The implementation of marketization in the public sector led to the negotiation between the state and society over their shares of social responsibility and, eventually, to a new definition of the relationship between the state and society, and between the public and the private domains. Therefore, the state was transformed from resource distributor to regulator and increasingly to market actor (Wu, Xu, & Yeh, 2007). In other words, the state became a developmental state while legitimizing itself by prioritizing development and combining the steady high rates of economic growth and structural change in the productive system, both domestically and in its relationship to the international economy (Castells, 2000).

Local autonomy and place promotion in Chinese cities

Along with the retreat of the state in the provision of capital for local development, alternative sources such as foreign investors and the domestic private sectors became the major source to support local economic development. To attract non-state capital, place promotion was carried out first at the national scale through the opening up of cities both economically and institutionally. In the early stages of reform, Special Economic Zones such as Shenzhen, Zhuhai, Xiamen, Shantou and Hainan were established to allow special economic policies, new systems of management and experiments on the land markets that encouraged and attracted non-state investment, especially foreign capital. Then in 1984 the policies were expanded to 14 Open Coastal Cities that were endowed with great autonomy in fiscal and management affairs.

These cities were selected as the first bunch for place promotion because the contribution of these far coastal areas to China's treasury was much less at that time, thus any failure on their part would not greatly upset the national budget and would not undermine the political authority in Beijing (Tian, 1996). In contrast, it was considered too great a risk to allow experiments to take place in cities like Shanghai that were dominant in the urban economic hierarchy. Besides, the reform initiative in the southeastern coastal provinces was also believed to benefit from their proximity to Hong Kong, Macau and Taiwan (Gu & Tang, 2002).

Place promotion of these cities proved to be a great success. They performed as catalysts for active trade and investment and expanded their vigour and influence into the surrounding regions. Therefore, the national strategy of place promotion was soon implemented in inland areas, following the same principles of gradualism as applied in the general economic reform programs. Open Economic Regions were established later in inland areas, with similar incentives in the Yangtze River Delta, Pearl River Delta and coastal Fujian. In the early 1990s, Pudong New Area was created in metropolitan Shanghai and became the new focus of major national and municipal initiatives and investment. At the same time many provincial capital cities and five cities along the Yangtze River were granted open city status. A national urban landscape including various tiers of cities came into being gradually.

The various levels of development priority in the setting up of Special Economic Zones and the open up of cities contributed to greater variations among various localities in terms of the level of fiscal effort, degree of economic advancement and provision of social services (Tong, 1989; T. Zhang & Zou, 2001). This brought about imbalance and larger gaps among cities as well as between the cities and the countryside, which gave rise to strong urban competition. Unlike the inter-city relations in the centrally planned system, competition among cities and between the cities and the rural economy today is no longer internalized and controlled by the central state because the vertical linkages have been loosened. It is up to local governments to smooth the horizontal linkages and interaction among cities as well as between the cities and the countryside.

With this pressure, local governments must endeavour to create a more competitive transactional environment and a more favourable place to win in the competition with other cities in attracting foreign investors and private sectors. This competition was also intensified by the government and party structures because in a non-elected government system, leaders were judged for promotion according to the development success of their current localities (Gu & Tang, 2002). This constitutes the local dimension of place promotion in Chinese cities. Promotional measures such as development zones, infrastructure improvement, prestige projects and land markets are adopted with the aim of using market instruments to manage state assets so as to generate a return on investment (Wu, 2009).

Large cities such as Shanghai and Beijing are generators of economic growth and have attracted more investment from both international corporations and domestic investors that are seeking better returns in large cities. Although China's official urban policies promote the development of small cities and discourage the growth of large cities, central government took a laissez-faire attitude toward the further expansion of large cities in practice and acknowledged their contributions to the national economy. Thus urban development and redevelopment projects in large cities were stimulated. Statistics revealed that the expansion of urbanized areas of large cities was faster than that of other cities, indicating that more development activities took place in large cities (T. W. Zhang, 2002). However in recent years, the population of small cities increased faster than that of large ones, a reflection of the official urban policy.

As a result, large-scale urban development has happened in all Chinese cities since the 1980s. By 1980, only 19.6% of the total population in China lived in urban areas, and investment in urban development was very limited (Pan & Wei, 2012). Since the economic reforms in urban areas, however, China has experienced rapid urbanization accompanied by fast economic growth. Urban population increased to 34% (691 million) in 1998, and the number of cities grew from 381 in 1987 to 668 in 1998, an increase of 75.3% in a decade (National Bureau of Statistics of China, 1999). By the end of 2011, the total urban population was 691 million in the mainland of China, accounting for 51.3% of the total. There were 30 cities with over eight million urban residents and 13 cities exceeded 10 million (Pan & Wei, 2012).

Restructuring the governance of universities into local plans

As the reforms began to take hold, it was soon discovered that the educational level of workers in China could not keep up with the fast development of the urban economy. The educational system controlled by the central government alone was woefully too rigid and management inefficient, especially for fast-growing cities. It would kill the initiatives and enthusiasm of the urban government if over-centralizing and stringent rules were preserved. Therefore, central government called for resolute steps to streamline educational administration and devolve powers to the units at lower levels so as to allow them more flexibility to run education and to fit into local development.

The promulgation of the *Decision on Reform of Educational System* in 1985 marks the first round of comprehensive reform in the Chinese higher education sector. The key to restructuring higher education was considered to lie in eliminating excessive government control over higher education institutions and, under the guidance of the policies and plans in education, extending the decision-making power of the colleges and universities and strengthening their ties with the production units, scientific research institutions and similar sectors, so that they will have the initiative and ability to serve economic and social development (Central Committee of the Communist Party of China, 1985). It puts the emphasis on local responsibility, multiple sources of educational funds, vocational and technical education, decentralization of power to individual institutions to govern their own affairs and diversity of educational opportunities. After the 1985 Decision, the State Education Commission, a counterpart of the Ministry of Education from 1985 to 1998, assumed just overall leadership to provide policy guidance and direction instead of routine management and administration over higher education (Mok, 2005).

The second round of educational reform began in 1993 when the *Outline for Reform and Development of Education in China* was issued. It realized the need to develop a better governance model to run and monitor higher education and proposed some key principles about how to restructure the relationship between the government and the university, between the central and the local, and between the State Education Commission and other central ministries so that the higher education system could be more compatible with the changing economic system (Central Committee of the Communist Party of China, 1993b). In 1995, the State Education Commission issued a policy document entitled *Suggestions on Deepening Higher Education Structural Reform*, recommending four major restructuring strategies, i.e. transferring, joint development, merging and cooperation, to reform the higher education system (State Education Commission, 1995). The essence of the policy was to decentralize the administration and financing of universities and to merge some universities to achieve economies of scale and economies of scope in terms of disciplines (Xue, 2006).

The large-scale management reform and governance change in China's higher education system was not implemented until 1998 when the central government carried out a major restructuring to abolish many industrial ministries. Before the education reform, the majority of universities were directly under different central ministries in order to train professional manpower for specific industries. With the abolition of some central ministries and the tendency toward decentralization in education reform, measures were adopted to change the leadership and governance structures in higher education. The leadership of the universities, originally led by different central ministries, was transferred to local governments so that better coordination among different local universities could be achieved. Universities were also given more autonomy in their day-to-day management. By 1999, there had been 226 universities in China transferred from different central ministries to education bureaus at the local level (Mok, 2005). After adopting the transferring strategy, the relationship between the State Education Commission, non-educational central ministries and local governments went through significant changes. These developments marked the new trend of localization of higher education in China.

Given the special features and the distinct roles of some institutions, especially those leading universities, a differentiated administering management model was introduced. These institutions were under joint development of the central and local governments, with the former prevailing in major decision-making and the latter prevailing in the daily management of the universities (State Education Commission, 1995). With the decentralization policies in place, especially the retreat of the non-educational central departments in higher education, local governments have strengthened their coordinating function and enhanced their financial responsibility in the higher education sector. Local government will place the universities under local economic and social development plans and provide funding for them; in return, the universities will, in their enrolment, curriculum design, graduates' employment, scientific research and so on, gear themselves to the need of local economic and social development (State Education Commission, 1995). Meanwhile, local governments have established a close cooperative relationship with the central ministries, largely the State Education Commission, to run and fund all leading universities located in their territories.

Moreover, the education reform also led to diversified educational services and a boom in private education. Generally speaking, there are three types of non-state higher education institutions in China and they adopt different strategies to run their colleges. The first is self-sufficient and primarily rely upon students' tuition fees or alumni funding to run the institutions; the second are financed partly by tuition fees and partly by the government or social institutions; the third adopt a private-run and public-assisted model and are financially supported by local government through a subsidized land price and/or staff salary payment (Mok, 2000). By 2012, there were 2,138 regular higher education institutions in China as acknowledged by the Ministry of Education, among which 403 were private institutions, accounting for 18.8% of the total (Ministry of Education of China, 2012). Although private educational institutions have become popular in China, they still face immense difficulties to compete with their formal counterparts. Knowing these dilemmas, the private colleges have a clear vision to differentiate themselves from the state-funded universities by specializing in courses that are geared to newly emerging market needs. In addition, they are committed to serve the local communities in which they are located, to establish a very close link with local enterprises to create more opportunities for its students to enrich their internship and placement experiences.

The changing role of universities in the Chinese regional innovation system

To promote the economic role of universities in local development, the Chinese government has taken further steps to incorporate universities into the national and regional innovation system. Typical measures include the cultivation of research universities, the promotion of university–industry linkages, the development of university-owned enterprises and the establishment of science parks.

Research universities

Studies on the determinants of national innovative capacity found that countries that have located a higher share of their research and development (R&D) activity in the educational sector, as opposed to the private sector or intramural government programs, have been able to achieve significantly higher patenting productivity (Furman, Porter, & Stern, 2002). To raise the research standards of universities, the central government in China introduced Project 211, attaching a new financial and strategic importance to selected universities to promote development in selected disciplines. On the heel of Project 211 was then launched Project 985 with the aim to turn top universities into world-class research universities. The universities are assessed by quantifiable and objective criteria such as staffing, buildings, libraries, laboratories and research to determine whether they are qualified to be designated. Competition for the designation was very fierce because the selected universities will receive substantial funding from central government to expand their research capacities and disciplinary scope, with matching funds from local government. By now there have been 116 universities listed in Project 211 and 39 universities in Project 985 (Figure 4.1).

Chinese universities perform as an important locus of R&D. They published 343,000, or 64.6% of all, domestic S&T papers in 2010. R&D

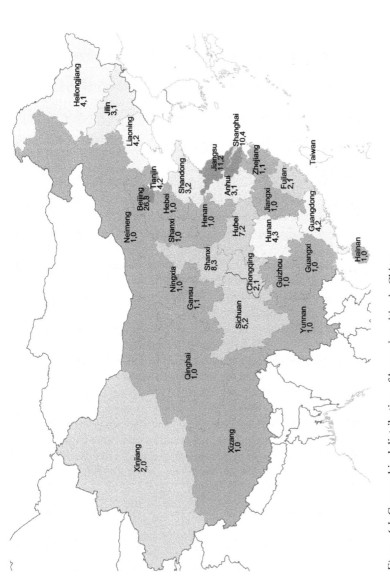

Figure 4.1 Geographical distribution of key universities in China

Source: (Ministry of Education of China, 2010, 2011); compiled by author.

Notes: The first number below the name of cities and regions refers to the number of universities in Project 211; the second number refers to those in Project 985.

personnel and expenditure in Chinese universities have been increasing year by year. In 2010, there were 290,000 R&D personnel in Chinese universities, 5.3% higher than in 2009. Their R&D expenditure reached 59.73 billion yuan in 2010, 27.6% more than in 2009 (Ministry of Science and Technology of China, 2012). However, the share of university R&D personnel and expenditure in the national total kept on decreasing because of the large number and rapid development of R&D activities in enterprises. The share of university R&D personnel had been decreased from 18.4% in 2004 to 11.3% in 2010. The share of university R&D expenditure kept around 10% from 2001 to 2005, but then continued to decrease for the next few years. In 2010, the share was only 8.5%.

Basic research has always been an important part of universities' R&D activities. In 2006, universities surpassed the research institutes in terms of basic research expenditure to become the largest think tank in China. Basic research expenditure in universities amounted to 17.99 billion yuan in 2010, 23.7% higher than in 2009, while the national rate was just 20%. The share of university basic research expenditure in the nation kept rising and reached 55.4% in 2010. The number of basic research personnel in universities amounted to 10,000 in 2010, accounting for 41.4% of the total R&D personnel in the universities and 69.1% of the total basic research personnel in China (Ministry of Science and Technology of China, 2012).

Despite the dominant role of universities in basic research, an examination of R&D activities of Chinese universities reveals that a very large proportion of their expenditure and personnel are involved in applied research and development because it is much easier to transfer applied research than basic research into high-tech industrialization. Since 1991, the share of applied research expenditure in the total R&D funds in universities and colleges stayed above 55% until the year 2000 when this share began to drop, but it still remained at over 50%. The share of personnel occupied in applied research in the total R&D personnel had also been over half. In 2011, 56.4% of the R&D personnel in Chinese universities were engaged in applied research, while 30.1% in basic research and 13.4% in experimental development (Ministry of Science and Technology of China, 2001–2011).

University–industry linkages

In 1999, the role of Chinese universities in the national innovation system was further strengthened by encouraging university–industry linkages through a legal framework – *Several Provisions on Promoting the Transformation of Scientific and Technological Achievements*. The 1999 Provisions was jointly released by seven central ministries and organizations and was approved by the State Council. It made generous allowance for rewarding discoverers of innovative and productive knowledge. Researchers making achievements may be rewarded no less than 20% of the after-tax income or stock from technology transfer. The primary researcher may gain no less than 50% of the total reward. The 1999 Provisions also made it easier for research personnel to move back and forth between research and business. There were also favourable policies about tax relief and intellectual property protection.

Encouraged by such policies, Chinese universities showed great potential in knowledge production and high-tech industrialization and became a main force in the national innovation system. The number of patents applied for by Chinese universities amounted to 79,332 in 2010, 28.8% more than in 2009 (Ministry of Science and Technology of China, 2012). Among those, 48,294 were inventions, 27.2% more than in 2009. In terms of those certified to universities, the number of patents was 43,153 in 2010, 54.5% more than in 2009, among which 19,036 were certified inventions, 32.3% more than in 2009. In 2001, the State Economic and Trade Commission and the Ministry of Education jointly set up the first group of state technology transfer centres in six universities to promote the commercialization of technological achievements. Technology transfer from university to industry was encouraged through licensing and other arrangements such as consulting, joint or contract R&D and technical services. The universities are building commercial linkages and there is an entrepreneurial bent to university administration. As a result, the contribution of enterprises in university funding grew rapidly, while government funding dropped from 80.35% in 1996 to 49.56% in 2004 (H. L. Yang, Yuan, & Chen, 2010). Since 2003, university R&D funding has remained a relatively stable structure, with 54–58% from government, 35–37% from enterprises and 7–10% from other domestic and foreign sources (Figure 4.2) (Ministry of Science and Technology of China, 2012).

University-owned enterprises

All the previous discussions about the role of Chinese universities in the national innovation system are familiar throughout the world. What is unique in the Chinese context are university-owned enterprises that are controlled by their affiliated universities in one way or another. The legitimacy of this control derives from the fact that many of these enterprises were created with funds from the university or by virtue of the credit or brand of the university. In some cases, enterprises willingly transfer their management control to universities so that they can generate intangible benefits for themselves. University-owned enterprises are the main sources through which Chinese universities engage in the market.

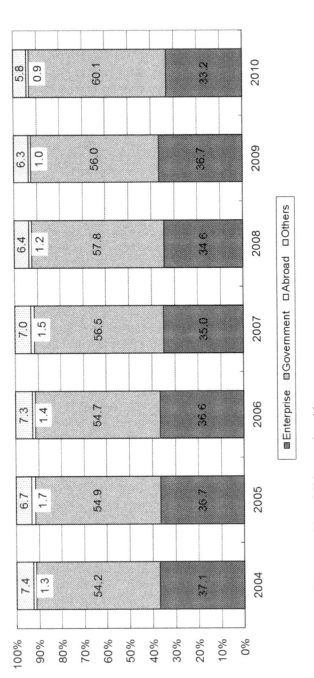

Figure 4.2 Funding composition of Chinese universities

Source: (Ministry of Science and Technology of China, 2005–2011); compiled by author.

University-owned enterprises are not new things for Chinese universities. Many Chinese universities, particularly those engineering and science-based universities, have had university-owned factories since the 1950s. These were mainly used for students to get short-term internships or apprenticeships in a real production environment. Also, under the 'work unit system', many Chinese universities had their own service providers such as print shops, publishers and guest-houses. What is different now is the new market environment, the new roles these enterprises are playing or expected to play and the complex relationships they have developed with their parent universities.

University-owned enterprises are currently generally run under three models. The first one is the university-owned service providers, such as factories or print shops; the second model is to bring university technologies to create joint commercial entities with enterprises outside universities; the third model is technology development companies created by universities and departments (Xue, 2006). Enterprises of the high-tech type are particularly encouraged. In 2004, there were 4,563 enterprises affiliated with universities in China, among which about 40% were involved in S&T activities (Xue, 2006). While the number was less than half of the total, these enterprises accounted for the majority of the total number in terms of sales, profit and tax paid almost every year. For example, in 2003 and 2004, over 80% of the sales were generated by these S&T enterprises (Xue, 2006). It is clear that S&T enterprises are the backbones of the university-owned enterprises.

Although many Chinese universities have university-owned enterprises, only a small number of them have really successful ones. Successful and influential university-owned enterprises are concentrated in a small number of selected universities and cities around the country. Statistics show that about 75% of the total sales, amounting to 70.57 billion yuan, realized by Chinese university-owned enterprises are concentrated in the top 20 universities (Xue, 2006). Analysis on these 20 parent universities found that contributors to the strong growth of university-owned enterprises include strong engineering research and talented faculty and students, academic strengths and reputation, unique comparative advantages such as well-known pharmaceutical and foreign language advantages (Xue, 2006).

Over the past several years, especially between 1998 and 2000, university-owned enterprises maintained their growth momentum in terms of sales, profits and tax. However, since 2001, the growth rate has slowed down to some extent (Xue, 2006). New controversies began to surface over the appropriateness of universities getting involved in running business enterprises. There were also concerns about the potential financial risks for universities that were linked to the university-owned enterprises that were traded on the stock markets. Further, more university-owned enterprises increasingly felt the need to change their governance structure so that they could operate like real commercial enterprises. Recently, the government has begun to encourage universities and their affiliated enterprises to 'de-link' by clarifying intellectual property rights and respective obligations, separating management from administration, reforming shareholding arrangements to establish a modern business system, and standardizing the operating quality and investment action to ensure scientific management. Clearly, university-owned enterprises in China are now at a new crossroads.

Science parks

The normal impact of R&D is important to improve the innovation capability of individual companies and institutions, but more important to promote urban economic development is whether the university and related firms are able to build knowledge networks around clusters of knowledge-intensive production units of goods and services (Audretsch, 1998; Huggins, 2008; Lambooy, 1996; Porter, 1998, 2000). Clusters are geographic concentrations of interconnected companies, specialized suppliers, service providers, universities and associated institutions in particular fields that compete but also cooperate (Porter, 2000). They affect urban economic development by increasing the productivity of companies, driving the direction and pace of innovation, stimulating the formation of new businesses, expanding and strengthening the cluster itself (Porter, 1998).

A university-based science park focuses on the intellectual and knowledge capital residing within and exchanged among individuals, firms, universities and other knowledge-creating institutions. Instead of a place for mass production, science parks are launched mainly to incubate spin-offs created by the faculty or students from universities, to provide a platform for new ideas produced elsewhere to be commercialized for the local market, and to provide services for the enterprises located in the science park. Universities provide specialized training, education, information, research and technical support for the science parks. And science parks provide a sound environment for innovation ranging from managing real estate to fundraising and from talent hunting to assuring legal arrangement.

China's science parks were inspired partly by the legends of Stanford Science Park, Cambridge Science Park, and many others. The first Chinese science park, and now the largest, was launched in 1988 at Zhongguancun, within the Beijing Experimental Zone (Macdonald & Deng, 2004). Since then, university-based science parks have become new avenues for commercializing university technologies and for catalyzing urban development zones. According to the statistics issued by the Science and Technology Development Centre of Ministry of Education, by 2010, there were 86 university-based science parks at the national level throughout China (Figure 4.3). Besides, there is also a large group of

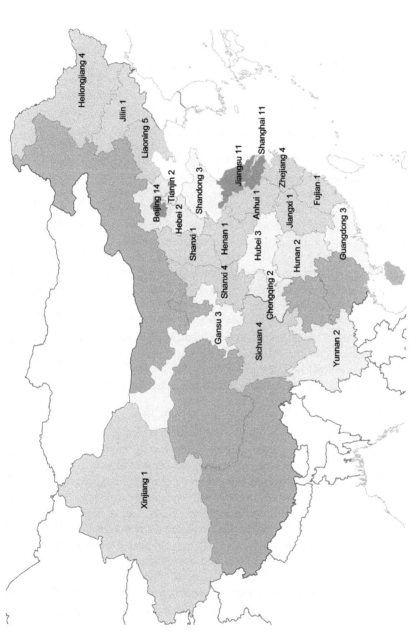

Figure 4.3 Geographical distribution of national level university-based science parks in China

Source: www.cutech.edu.cn/cn/index.htm; compiled by author.

university-based science parks launched by local governments or independently organized by universities themselves. Most of these parks are located in or adjacent to the university campus and administered by a commercial entity established by the university or through a joint venture between local government and the university. As an important part of the innovation system, a successful science park has become the symbol of a top-class university. They not only help regional economic development by fostering the growth of high-tech enterprises and boosting technology innovation, but also provide an important platform for the university to serve society. In 2004, out of 4,563 university-owned enterprises in China, 24.57% were located in science parks. Although in the minority, these enterprises performed much better than the off-park enterprises in terms of income, profit and tax paid (Xue, 2006).

Those science parks that were independent of the universities at the initial stage of their development would also like to collaborate with universities after they were on track. For example, Zhangjiang High-Tech Park, with specialized research in life sciences, software and information technology, was set up in Pudong New Area, isolated from the many universities in central Shanghai. It soon attracted Fudan University, Shanghai Jiaotong University, and Shanghai University of Traditional Chinese Medicine to establish branch campuses in the science park by providing free land and lucrative collaborative opportunities. The current Zhangjiang High-Tech Park is made up of the following areas: Technical Innovation Area, Hi-Tech Industry Area, Scientific Research and Education Area, and Residential Area. Education and research provided by the universities have become an indispensable part for the innovation and industrial production in the science park.

Science parks facilitate the production, distribution and application of science and technology by providing the space in which government, universities, and enterprises work together and creating environments that foster cooperation and innovation. An evolved form of science parks, i.e. the strategically planned mixed-use campus expansion, is emerging and involves shared space in which industry and academic researchers can work side by side. These university-affiliated mixed-use campus developments are not simply real-estate ventures. They embody a commitment by universities to partake in broader activities, offering companies high-value sites for accessing researchers, specialized facilities and students, and promoting live–work–play environments. Key features of these mixed-use developments include space for significant future research growth, multi-tenant facilities to house researchers and companies, and housing, along with other amenities that are attractive to young faculty, post-doctoral and graduate students.

University–city coalitions with deliberate institutional ambiguity

With the objective of improving urban economic performance as well as strengthening the combination of education, scientific research and social application, the universities got development incentives and were affected by strong market forces. The engagement of universities in the market takes two distinct forms: the first involves attempts to market their academic wares in the commercial world; while the other is to restructure universities in terms of business principles and practices (Buchbinder & Newson, 1990). Therefore, the institutional role of universities begins to change: officially an academic institution, the universities are increasingly incorporated into the economic agenda of the state with emphasis on the importance of market dynamics.

The market is the very locus that can help ease the tension between the university and the city. In comparison with the centralized planning and hierarchical system in which interaction between the cities and the universities was manipulated by the central state, decentralized reform has strengthened the power of cities and granted more autonomy to universities. Both the universities and the cities got development incentives and were affected by strong market forces. The diffused entrepreneurship leads to a recognized set of codes of conduct, support, and practices that both the university and the local government can dip into. It also provides an opportunity for them to make joint effort so as to attain the common goal of economic development.

Therefore we see various development coalitions among the university, the government, the industry and other related important actors. They are represented by a number of hybrid organizations. Hybrids encompass a broad range of organizational combinations of various sizes, shapes and purposes, some of which are formal organization, some are formalized relationships but not proper organizations, whereas others are informal relationships. Several hybrid types can be identified in the politics of university–city interaction: mergers unifying two or more universities into a single one, joint governance among multi-level governments, cooperative agreements involving collaborative programs among university–government–industry, joint ventures resulting in the creation of a new company that is formally independent of the parents such as spin-off companies in science parks.

Hybrid organizations can mobilize resources and/or governance structures from more than one existing organization (Borys & Jemison, 1989), and they are capable of reducing uncertainty in inter-organizational relationships involving bilateral dependency (Pfeffer, 1972; Pfeffer & Nowak, 1976). Governed by hybrid organizations, the universities develop their properties with strategies to mix proprietary and academic uses and engage in the construction of cities by producing whole zones of development in the form of science parks; the enterprises participate in joint R&D and publications, contract research, sharing research labs, licensing, technology sales and so on, and contribute to technological innovation and application; the governments facilitate the process by providing land or special revenues and establishing institutionalized channels for market-oriented activities.

The coalitions on the basis of entrepreneurship, however, are not permanent and stable; they are based on the priority of projects. Among various projects encouraged, those that can suit the needs of the market are especially supported. For example, science parks were promoted largely because they provide a common ground where the universities get space for knowledge commercialization, the enterprises find intellectual and institutional support, and the cities get a catalyst for industrial upgrading. The strategies of the coalition are adjusted constantly according to the particular requirements of the project. When the project is accomplished, the coalition may be dissolved.

Besides, the overlapping institutional spheres embedded in hybrid organizations may easily induce institutional ambiguity. For example, universities in China enjoy some privilege in obtaining land use rights at 'allocation prices' that are much lower than 'conveyance prices' paid by commercial users. They are not allowed to make a profit on the land obtained through allocation. However, by transferring land use rights from the university to university-owned enterprises at a 'negotiated price', it is possible for the land to be circulated in the market. It is for the benefit of the pro-growth coalition but at the expense of state revenue and public interest. Hybrid organizations may also end up with bad debts because of over-investment and poor management in the process of university spatial development. These bad debts are usually referred to as 'triangular debt' because they involve at least three parties, such as the university, the enterprises and the banks, which are all affiliated to the same organization, usually the state. Consequently, no one knows who should take the ultimate responsibility because they all belong to and work for the same one. There have also been occasions when some of these hybrid organizations or companies ran into bad debts and central and local government have taken a hands-off approach and refused to rescue them. The governments therefore escape the responsibility of sharing the risks of the coalition.

In China, higher education reforms are designed only to improve productivity and enhance economic efficiency. It has never been in the central planners' minds to replace the centrally planned system with a capitalist market economy but rather to make the planning system more flexible and decentralized. The reforms are used as an instrument to legitimate rather than to undermine the existing political structure. The only change was that socialist pragmatism substituted for socialist idealism, of which socialism and associated state ownership are still the cornerstones (Zhu, 1999). Therefore, the potential of the higher education system for effecting social change has never been seen by the state as a relatively autonomous social institution to ultimately address social ills in the larger society, but was rather regarded as a mere apparatus within the state and often becomes an instrument for furthering the interests of those in power (Tsang, 2000).

References

Audretsch, D. B. (1998). Agglomeration and the location of innovative activity. *Oxford Review of Economic Policy, 14*(2), 18–29.

Borys, B., & Jemison, D. B. (1989). Hybrid arrangements as strategic alliances: Theoretical issues in organizational combinations. *Academy of Management Review, 14*(2), 234–249.

Brenner, N. (2004). *New State Spaces: Urban Governance & the Rescaling of Statehood*. New York: Oxford University Press.

Buchbinder, H., & Newson, J. (1990). Corporate-university linkages in Canada: Transforming a public institution. *Higher Education, 20*(4), 355–379.

Castells, M. (2000). *The Rise of the Network Society*. Malden, MA: Blackwell.

Central Committee of the Communist Party of China. (1985). *Decision of the Central Committee of the Communist Party of China on Reform of Educational System*.

Central Committee of the Communist Party of China. (1993a). *Decision of the Central Committee of the Communist Party of China on Some Issues Concerning the Establishment of the Socialist Market Economy*.

Central Committee of the Communist Party of China. (1993b). *Outline for Reform and Development of Education in China*.

Central Committee of the Communist Party of China. (2003). *Decision of the Central Committee of the Communist Party of China on Some Issues Concerning the Improvement of the Socialist Market Economy*.

Flynn, N. (1997). *Public Sector Management*. Hempstead: Harvester Wheatsheaf.

Furman, J. L., Porter, M. E., & Stern, S. (2002). The determinants of national innovative capacity. *Research Policy, 31*(6), 899–933.

Gu, F. R., & Tang, Z. (2002). Shanghai: Reconnecting to the Global Economy. In S. Sassen (Ed.), *Global Networks, Linked Cities*. New York: Routledge.

Hawkins, J. N. (2000). Centralization, decentralization, recentralization: Educational reform in China. *Journal of Educational Administration, 38*(5), 442–455.

Hood, C. (1991). A public management for all seasons? *Public Administration, 69*(1), 3–19.

Huggins, R. (2008). The evolution of knowledge clusters: Progress and policy. *Economic Development Quarterly, 22*(4), 277–289.

Jin, H., Qian, Y., & Weingast, B. R. (2005). Regional decentralization and fiscal incentives: Federalism, Chinese style. *Journal of Public Economics, 89*(9–10), 1719–1742.

Kooiman, J. (1993). *Modern Governance: New Government–Society Interactions.* London: Sage.

Lambooy, J. G. (1996). Knowledge production, organisation and agglomeration economies. *Geojournal, 41*(41), 293–300.

Lin, J. Y., & Liu, Z. (1998). Fiscal decentralization and economic growth in China. *Social Science Electronic Publishing, 49*(1), 1–21.

Liu, Z., & Zhou, Y. (Producer). (2008, 20 November 2012). *National Bureau of Statistics of China: China's GDP Accounting for 6% of the World.* Retrieved from http://news.xinhuanet.com/fortune/2008-10/27/content_10259186.htm.

Macdonald, S., & Deng, Y. (2004). Science parks in China: A cautionary exploration. *International Journal of Technology Intelligence & Planning, 1*(1), 1–14.

McGee, T. G., Lin, G. C. S., Marton, A. M., Wang, M. Y. L., & Wu, J. (2007). *China's Urban Space: Development under Market Socialism.* London and New York: Routledge.

Ministry of Education of China. (2010). *List of Universities in '211 Project'.*

Ministry of Education of China. (2011). *List of Universities in '985 Project'.*

Ministry of Education of China. (2012). *List of Private Universities Approved by Ministry of Education.*

Ministry of Science and Technology of China. (2001–2011). *China Science and Technology Statistics.*

Ministry of Science and Technology of China. (2005–2011). *China Science and Technology Statistics.*

Ministry of Science and Technology of China. (2012). *Analysis on R&D Activities of Chinese Universities in 2010. (No. 514).* Retrieved from www.sts.org.cn/tjbg/gdxx/documents/2011/20120214.htm

Mok, K. H. (1997). Privatization or marketization: Educational development in post-Mao China. *International Review of Education, 43*(5–6), 547–567.

Mok, K. H. (2000). Marketizing higher education in post-Mao China. *International Journal of Educational Development, 20*(2), 109–126.

Mok, K. H. (2005). Globalization and educational restructuring: University merging and changing governance in China. *Higher Education, 50*(1), 57–88.

Morris, J., Hassard, J., & Sheehan, J. (2002). Privatization, Chinese-style: Economic reform and the state-owned enterprises. *Public Administration, 80*(80), 359–373.

National Bureau of Statistics of China. (1999). *China Statistical Yearbook 1999.* Beijing: China Statistical Publishing House.

Oi, J. C. (1992). Fiscal reform and the economic foundations of local state corporatism in China. *World Politics, 45*(1), 99–126.

Pan, J., & Wei, H. (Eds.). (2012). *Blue Book of Cities in China: Annual Report on Urban Development of China, No. 5.* Beijing: Social Sciences Academic Press.

Peters, B. G., & Pierre, J. (1998). Governance without government? Rethinking public administration. *Journal of Public Administration Research & Theory, 8*(2), 223–243.

Pfeffer, J. (1972). Merger as a response to organizational interdependence. *Administrative Science Quarterly, 17*(3), 382–394.

Pfeffer, J., & Nowak, P. (1976). Joint ventures and interorganizational interdependence. *Administrative Science Quarterly, 21*(3), 398–418.

Porter, M. E. (1998). Clusters and the new economics of competition. *Harvard Business Review, 76*(6), 77–90.

Porter, M. E. (2000). Location, competition, and economic development: Local clusters in a global economy. *Economic Development Quarterly, 14*(1), 15–34.

Rhodes, R. A. W. (1997). *Understanding Governance: Policy Networks, Governance, Reflexivity and Accountability*. Maidenhead and Philadelphia: Open University Press.

Rosenau, J. N., & Czempiel, E. (Eds.). (1992). *Governance without Government: Order and Change in World Politics*. Cambridge: Cambridge University Press.

State Council of China. (1980). *Decision of the State Council of the People's Republic of China on the Implementation of the Fiscal System with 'Separate Categories of Taxes, Expenditures and Responsibility Contracts at Various Levels'*.

State Council of China. (1985). *Decision of the State Council of the People's Republic of China on the Implementation of the Fiscal System with 'Separate Categories of Taxes, Designated Scope of Revenues, and Expenditures and Responsibility Contracts at Various Levels'*.

State Council of China. (1988). *Decision of the State Council of the People's Republic of China on Measures concerning the Implementation of Local Fiscal Responsibility*.

State Education Commission. (1995). *Suggestions on Deepening Higher Education Structural Reform*.

Tian, G. (1996). *Shanghai's Role in the Economic Development of China: Reform of Foreign Trade and Investment*. Westport: Praeger Publishers.

Tong, J. (1989). Fiscal Reform, Elite Turnover and Central-Provincial Relations in Post-Mao China. *Australian Journal of Chinese Affairs, 22*(22), 1–28.

Tsang, M. C. (2000). Education and national development in China since 1949: Oscillating policies and enduring dilemmas. *Economics of Education Review,* 579–618.

Weingast, B. R., Qian, Y., & Montinola, G. (1995). Federalism, Chinese style: The political basis for economic success in China. *World Politics, 48*(1), 50–81.

Wong, C. P. W. (1991). Central–Local relations in an era of fiscal decline: The paradox of fiscal decentralization in post-Mao China. *China Quarterly, 128*(128), 691–715.

Wu, F. (2009). Globalization, the Changing State, and Local Governance in Shanghai. In X. Chen & Z. Zhou (Eds.), *Shanghai Rising: State Power and Local Transformations in a Global Megacity*. Minneapolis and London: University of Minnesota Press.

Wu, F., Xu, J., & Yeh, A. G. O. (2007). *Urban Development in Post-Reform China: State, Market, and Space*. Oxon and New York: Routledge.

Xue, L. (2006). *Universities in China's National Innovation System*. Paper presented at the UNESCO Forum on Higher Education, Research and Knowledge, Paris, France.

Yang, H. L., Yuan, S. J., & Chen, M. (2010). Evolution, characteristics and developing countermeasures of China's higher education fiscal system since the reform and opening up. *Journal of Hebei University, 35*(3), 76–82.

Yang, J. (2011). *Development of the Non-State Sector in China: An Update.* EAI Background Brief No. 606.

Zhang, T., & Zou, H. F. (2001). Fiscal decentralization, public spending, and economic growth in China. *Journal of Public Economics, 67*(2), 221–240.

Zhang, T. W. (2002). Urban development and a socialist pro-growth coalition in Shanghai. *Urban Affairs Review, 37*(4), 475–499.

Zhu, J. (1999). *The Transition of China's Urban Development: From Plan-Controlled to Market-Led.* Westport: Praeger Publishers.

5 University development and urban restructuring in Shanghai

It is evident that the state served as the initial trigger for and sustained a strong influence on China's market reforms and opening up, and that nationwide reforms were responsible for creating an environment in which university–city relations are being restructured. Deeply embedded in the national environment, university–city interactions differentiate a lot across cities. A crucial factor influencing university activities is the underlying development needs, conditions, and priorities of the city. Shanghai as China's leading metropolis has been undertaking urban development in an advanced stage compared with other Chinese cities. There are more evident and urgent needs for higher education in Shanghai along with the knowledge-drive urban socio-economic restructuring. Shanghai's universities are therefore facing more severe challenges such as the growing number of students, the shortage of university facilities, and the need to enhance the quality of education. At the same time, the simultaneous occurrence of inner city renewal and suburbanization in Shanghai exert complex challenges for universities as they occupy a large quantity of land and buildings. The universities have to seek opportunities for self-development and to reconsider their relations with the city.

This chapter will explore the changing relations between the universities and the city in Shanghai in the process of urban socio-economic restructuring and urban spatial restructuring. First, it will analyze the urban development modes of Shanghai in the post-reform era. Then it will examine the increasing importance of higher education in the urban socio-economic restructuring process. After that, it will explore how university expansion is carried out as a consequence of the massification of higher education. Next will be discussed the engagement of universities in urban spatial restructuring. Finally there is some reflection on the concept of 'urban university', i.e. the debates on the university 'of' the city versus the university 'in' the city.

Urban development modes of Shanghai

Before 1978

Throughout its history, the urban development of Shanghai has always revolved around its role as an economic centre. Initially a seaport and fishing town of only local importance, its designation as a treaty port in 1842 produced a turnaround in Shanghai's economic fortunes. It soon grew into a strong industrial centre, producing textiles, flour and tobacco, and became an international trade port. Between 1860 and 1930, 68% of the total value of Chinese trade passed through Shanghai, while by 1936 it handled half of China's foreign trade (Gu & Tang, 2002). The penetration of foreign capital sped up industrialization and led to the prospering of local industrial entrepreneurs in Shanghai and its environs. Shanghai performed as a channel through which foreign products were distributed to the region and at the same time domestic agricultural and mineral products were processed and exported.

After 1949, the turn toward centralized planning and the placing of increasing emphasis on heavy industry, regional self-sufficiency and minimal reliance on foreign trade began to transform the character of China's large coastal cities, in particular Shanghai. Service functions such as trade, finance, and distribution dwindled. No longer an international city, Shanghai, for the first time in history, developed a comprehensive industrial system, including heavy industries (F. Wu, 2009). Although the degree of concentration of industrial, financial, and trading capacity in Shanghai was dissipated in the Maoist period, Shanghai still remained China's leading metropolis through to 1978. In the 1970s, Shanghai's industrial output accounted for one-seventh of the national total; its fiscal revenue was about one-fourth to one-sixth of the national total; and the volume of freight handled and the value of export goods were about one-third of the national total (F. Wu, 2009). In the heyday of socialist development, Shanghai was also the source of innovation and production capacity.

1978–1990

With the start of China's reforms in 1978, the experiment of opening up and market economy was initiated in the Special Economic Zones of Guangdong and Fujian Provinces. Given Shanghai's dominance of the urban economic hierarchy, it was considered too great a risk to allow experiments to take place in Shanghai. Lacking the incentive structures of the Special Economic Zones, Shanghai became marginalized in the new race for investment and growth. On the other side, it was imperative for the central state to impose a strict fiscal policy on Shanghai because Shanghai made a heavy contribution to the national revenues: between 1949 and 1980, roughly 86% of Shanghai's revenue was remitted to central government (Yusuf & Wu, 1997). So when the central authorities introduced a new decentralizing fiscal regime, under which the participating provinces were allowed a fixed and an adjustable share of revenues, Shanghai was largely, if not totally, bypassed during this first round of reforms. This served to hold back Shanghai's development throughout 1980s.

After 1990

The opening of Pudong New Area as a special development zone in 1990 proved to be the catalyst for Shanghai's rapid urban and economic transformation. Since some important leaders such as President Jiang Zemin and Premier Zhu Rongji serving in the central government of China rose to prominence in connection to the Shanghai municipal administration, the importance of Shanghai to national development was gradually accepted by central government and Shanghai was able to retain a larger proportion of revenues to invest in urban and economic development. It was repositioned as China's leading metropolis. Shanghai's official mission is to become the 'dragon head' of the Chinese economy and to become the 'three centres', namely, a financial centre, a trading centre and an economic centre. Due to Shanghai's strategic location, the abundant skilled manpower and highly favourable national policies, few doubt that Shanghai will soon recover its pre-war dominance as the centre of China's economy.

The opening of Pudong New Area not only provided the main impetus for Shanghai's dominance in the national economy, but also led to Shanghai's reintegration into the global economy. Improved transportation links, telecommunications networks and a web of international firms, including many large multinationals, are providing the infrastructure for the urban interface with global and regional systems (Zhou & Chen, 2009). Foreign investment to Shanghai, especially foreign direct investment, has risen rapidly (Gu & Tang, 2002; Tian, 1996; F. Wu, 2009; J. Wu, 2008). Socio-political ties, including tourism, educational visits, twinning arrangements, political and cultural exchanges, and government-sponsored trade affairs, which are increasing in number and frequency, provided an additional means of linkage between Shanghai and other cities regionally and globally. A steadily increasing number of foreign institutions, such as the World Bank and the Asian Development Bank, are also involved in the urban development of Shanghai.

Knowledge-driven socio-economic transformation in Shanghai

Shanghai has been undergoing dramatic socio-economic restructuring since the 1990s. Its development mode has been gradually shifted from the dominance of physical wealth to the leading of information and service industries such as communications, advertising, journalism, consulting, technology, patents, commercial, financial, insurance, real estate and tourism. The tertiary sector has been put pride of place. Knowledge plays an important role and performs as the driving force in this process. As a result, higher education has become a strategic field to promote rapid economic development to achieve higher social mobility.

Higher education as a lever of economic development

As we look back at two full decades of remarkable economic reform and social change in Shanghai beginning in the 1990s, we are struck by how fast Shanghai has developed. The average growth of Shanghai's GDP between 1990 and 2010 was 16.7%; GDP per capita rose from 5,911 yuan (1,236 US dollars) in 1990 to 76,074 yuan (11,238 US dollars) in 2010 (Shanghai Municipal Statistics Bureau, 2011b). As GDP increased, people's consumption ability was greatly promoted. The average disposable income per capita of urban households increased from 2,183 yuan in 1990 to 31,838 yuan in 2010, while the consumption expenditure per capita rose from 1,937 yuan to 23,200 yuan. From 1990 to 2010, expenditure on food (-23.0%), clothing (-3.0%) and household facilities (-2.3%) were substantially decreased; in contrast, more was spent on traffic and communications (+14.6%), residence (+4.6%), medical care (+3.7%), education and recreation (+2.6%) (Shanghai Municipal Statistics Bureau, 2011b).

Correspondingly, a marked structural and sectoral transition has appeared in Shanghai. During the past decade, the tertiary industry increased substantially and overtook the secondary industry to become the largest. The contribution of the tertiary industry to GDP rose from 31.9% in 1990 to 57.3% in 2010, while the secondary industry dropped from 63.8% to 42.1% (Shanghai Municipal Statistics Bureau, 2011b). In addition, the employment rate in manufacturing decreased whereas that in the service sectors enlarged. For example, comparing the occupation structure in 1990 with that in 2010, the most discernible changes of the employment rate lay in 'workers in manufacturing-related sectors' (-15.9%), 'sales and service people' (+13.4%), and 'staff and related people' (+7.7%), along with a slight increase of 'technical related staffs' (+1.7%) and 'administrators' (+1.5%) (Shanghai Municipal Statistics Bureau, 2011b).

In detail, the most evident increase in the tertiary industry of Shanghai appeared at both the higher ends, i.e. the sectors of finance, insurance and real estate, and the lower ends, i.e. the sectors of daily service. Statistics show a bimodal pattern of change in the economic structure of Shanghai from 1990 to 2000 (Figure 5.1): while the sector of 'finance and insurance' increased most dramatically in the first decade by 5.7% but then began to decease in the second decade, the contribution of 'real estate' increased by 5.3%; meanwhile, the contribution of 'retail, wholesale, hoteling and catering' to GDP increased by 9.8% and that of 'resident service, business service and public facility management' increased by 3.9% (Shanghai Municipal Statistics Bureau, 2011b). The five sub-sectors of transport and communication, retail and wholesale, finance and insurance, real estate, and daily service contributed to nearly half (48.6%) of Shanghai's GDP in 2010 (Shanghai Municipal Statistics Bureau, 2011b).

At the same time, the secondary industry of Shanghai has been upgraded. In particular, the gross output value of secondary industries with advanced technology increased while that of traditional industries decreased (Figure 5.2). Changes are especially pronounced in three sectors: communication and electronic equipment (+12.6%), transport equipment (+10.1%), and textiles (-11.1%). The six key industries of electronic information product manufacturing, automobile manufacturing, petrochemical and fine chemical products manufacturing, fine steel manufacturing, equipment complex manufacturing and bio-medicine manufacturing accounted for 66.1% of the total gross output value and concentrated 36.4% of employees in the secondary industry of Shanghai (Shanghai Municipal Statistics Bureau, 2011b).

Generally speaking, several features can be perceived in the economic restructuring of Shanghai. First, as national incomes rise, the proportion of money devoted to food at home begins to drop, and the marginal increments are used first for durables such as clothing, housing and automobiles and then for luxury items, recreation and the like. Second, in the very development of industry there is a necessary expansion of transportation and of public utilities, which work as auxiliary services in the movement of goods and the increasing use of energy, and an increase in the non-manufacturing but still blue-collar force. Third, in the mass consumption of goods and the growth of populations there is an increase in the wholesale and retail sectors and the finance, insurance and real estate sectors, which are the traditional centres of white-collar employment. These features correspond with the transformation from an industrial society to a knowledge society (Bell, 1999). In fact, it can be considered that Shanghai is in the transition from investment-driven to innovation-driven economic growth (Zhang, 2009).

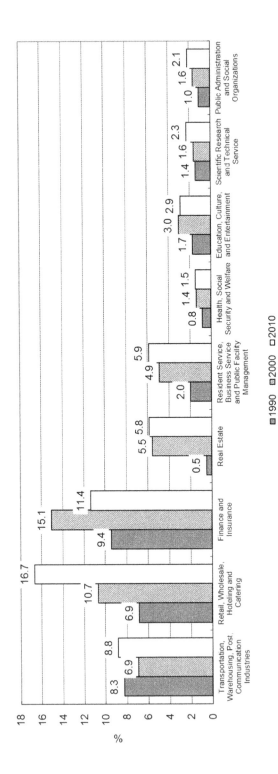

Figure 5.1 GDP contribution of tertiary sub-sectors in Shanghai, 1990–2010, %

Source: (Shanghai Municipal Statistics Bureau, 1991, 2001, 2011b); compiled by author.

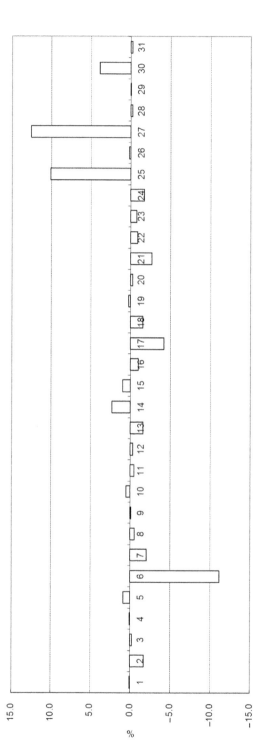

Figure 5.2 Changes in the composition of gross output value in secondary sub-sectors of Shanghai, 1990–2010, %

Source: (Shanghai Municipal Statistics Bureau, 1991, 2001, 2011b); compiled by author.

Note: Data used in 1990 and 2000 are Gross Output Value; data used in 2010 are Sales Value.

1, nonmetal mineral exploiting. 2, food manufacturing. 3, beverage manufacturing. 4, farm and sideline products processing. 5, tobacco manufacturing. 6, textile. 7, garments, shoes and accessories manufacturing. 8, leather, fur, and wool products manufacturing. 9, timber processing and timber, bamboo, rattan, coir and straw products manufacturing. 10, furniture manufacturing. 11, paper-making and paper products manufacturing. 12, printing and record duplicating. 13, stationary, education, sports goods, and artworks manufacturing. 14, oil processing, coking and nuclear fuel processing. 15, raw chemical materials and chemical products manufacturing. 16, medicine manufacturing. 17, chemical fiber manufacturing. 18, rubber products manufacturing. 19, plastic products manufacturing. 20, nonmetal mineral products. 21, smelting and pressing of ferrous metals. 22, smelting and pressing of nonferrous metals. 23, metal products manufacturing. 24, equipment manufacturing. 25, transportation equipment manufacturing. 26, electric machinery equipment and manufacturing. 27, communications equipment, computer and other electronic equipment manufacturing. 28, instruments, metres, culture and office equipment manufacturing. 29, production and supply of water. 30, production and supply of electricity, gas and thermal power. 31, other manufacture industry.

Higher education as a promoter of social mobility

Economic restructuring in Shanghai posed a requirement to encourage scholarship throughout society, to profoundly raise educational attainment and hence to improve labour quality. To meet rising market demand, Shanghai aims to build a so-called 'intellectual highland', to transform into a top-ranking international metropolis with the best talents nurtured by a top-ranking education system. It also echoes the state's developmental strategy of developing a knowledge-based society. Therefore, a series of policies has been promulgated by Shanghai municipality to upgrade educational attainment.

A typical case is the policy of urban household registration. In large and important cities such as Shanghai and Beijing, the registered population is strictly controlled through household registration system. People holding the urban household in these cities can enjoy lots of invisible benefits such as better welfare and job opportunities. Shanghai municipal authorities allow those with higher education or special talents larger quotas for urban household registration. For example, for students graduating from colleges outside Shanghai, only those holding 'a degree above or equal to a Master's degree, or a Bachelor's degree from colleges/universities located in Shanghai, or from colleges/universities developed by the State Council, or from those local colleges within 211 projects' are qualified to apply for Shanghai urban household registration (Shanghai Career Guidance Center for Graduates, 2001). The poor-educated and low-skilled, in contrast, have to go through a long and complicated process to remain legally in Shanghai (Li & Wu, 2006).

All these endeavors are intended to achieve an improvement in workforce quality. Consequently, there is a trend of progressively improving educational attainment in Shanghai. From 1990 to 2010, people with 'university and above' education substantially increased by 15.77%, while those with 'junior school' and 'senior school' education remained slightly increased and those with 'primary school' education or were 'semi-illiterate and below' dramatically decreased by 10.43% and 9.88% (Shanghai Municipal Statistics Bureau, 2011a). The total population with 'university and above' education in Shanghai was 5.04 million in 2010, 2.8 times that in 2000, among which those with technical, bachelor, and master degrees in 2010 was 2.37, 3.06, and 5.54 times respectively that in 2000 (Shanghai Municipal Statistics Bureau, 2011a).

The distribution of the higher educated in Shanghai shows typical features of concentration. Geographically, among the 5.04 million with 'university and above' education, nearly half were concentrated in Pudong New Area, Minhang District, Yangpu District and Xuhui District. In particular,

Pudong New Area attracted 1.10 million (21.92%). Comparing the share of higher educated in the total population, Xuhui District was the highest, reaching 38.5% in 2010, compared with the urban average of 22.82% (Shanghai Municipal Statistics Bureau, 2011a). The geographical distribution of the higher educated in Shanghai was highly influenced by the location of higher education institutions and central business district (CBD), the functional orientation and population amount in the area, and so on. Sectorally, about two-thirds of those with 'university and above' education were concentrated in the six sectors of manufacturing, retail and wholesale, education, leasing and business service, transportation, warehousing and post-industries, and finance (Shanghai Municipal Statistics Bureau, 2011a). Considering the share of higher educated in each sector (Figure 5.3), the most highly ranked were finance (80%), information and computer service (79.1%), scientific research and technical services (75.5%), education (73.6%), health and social security (58.1%), and public administration (57.8%), while the least ranked were farming (1.7%), residency services (6.7%), and hoteling and catering (11.6%) (Shanghai Municipal Statistics Bureau, 2011a).

The relationship between education and income has also become stronger. While it is not possible to compare the distribution of educational attainment among different income groups, as the statistics data does not cover this, the average compensation of employees in various sectors, however, provides a basis for cross-comparison. Employees in the sector of finance enjoyed the highest salaries, more than three times the social average and 1.68 times the second highest group, i.e. the sector of power production. The following were sectors of information and computer service, public administration, scientific research and technical service, health and social security, and education. The lowest income groups were residency services, hoteling and catering, and farming. In general, the income level in different sectors corresponds with their educational attainment (Figure 5.4), except the relatively higher income in the sector of power production, largely due to the state monopoly in energy control.

Higher education plays an important role in changing the social composition of the highest earning and status jobs. People with higher education have seen large increases in productivity and pay: they are more likely to be employed, more likely to enjoy higher wages and better job satisfaction, and more likely to move from one job to the next. In contrast, those with lower education have experienced reduced demand for their labour and lower wages. Higher education provides an access through which individuals from low-income backgrounds can enter higher status jobs and increase their earnings. It ensures that every person, regardless of their background, their circumstances, or their social class, has an equal opportunity to get on in life, especially in such a knowledge-based society. Higher education has

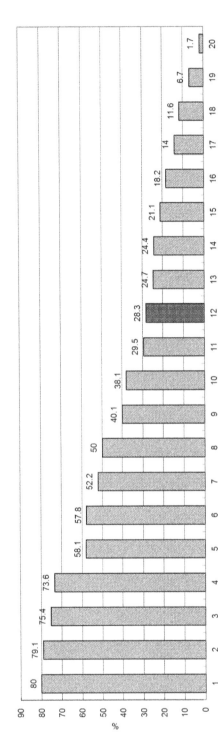

Figure 5.3 The share of people with 'university and above' education in different sectors in Shanghai, 2010

Source: (Shanghai Municipal Statistics Bureau, 2011a); compiled by author.

Note: 1, finance. 2, information transmission, computer service and software industries. 3, scientific research, technical service and geological prospecting. 4, education. 5, health, social security and welfare. 6, public administration and social organizations. 7, leasing and business service industries. 8, mining. 9, culture, sports and entertainment. 10, power, gas and water production and supply. 11, real estate. 12, average. 13, retail and wholesale. 14, transportation, warehousing and post industries. 15, manufacturing. 16, water conservancy, environment and public facility management. 17, construction. 18, hoteling and catering. 19, resident service and other services. 20, farming, forestry, animal husbandry and fishery.

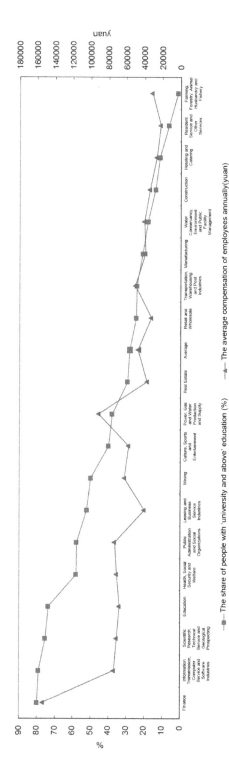

Figure 5.4 Educational attainment and income level in different sectors in Shanghai, 2010

Source: (Shanghai Municipal Statistics Bureau, 2011a, 2011b); compiled by author.

Legend:

— The share of people with 'university and above' education (%)

— The average compensation of employees annually(yuan)

Categories (x-axis): Finance; Information Transmission, Computer Service and Software Industries; Scientific Research, Technical Service and Geological Prospecting; Education; Health, Social Security and Welfare; Public Administration and Social Organizations; Leasing and Business Service Industries; Mining; Culture, Sports and Entertainment; Power, Gas and Water Production and Supply; Real Estate; Average; Retail and Wholesale; Transportation, Warehousing and Post Industries; Manufacturing; Water Conservancy Environment and Public Facility Management; Construction; Hotelling and Catering; Resident Service and Other Services; Farming, Forestry, Animal Husbandry and Fishery become a strategic means to promote social mobility, to keep vibrancy of the economy, to move towards high-value goods, services and industries, and to maintain a competitive edge.

University expansion as a consequence of mass higher education

The increasing importance of higher education has led to increasing enrolment in universities. From 2000 to 2010, the number of higher education institutions in Shanghai increased from 37 to 66 and the number of students increased from 226,800 to 515,700. At the same time, the number of enrolled students increased from 81,300 in 2000 to 144,600 in 2010, with the enrolment ratio rising from 67.4% to 85.1% (Shanghai Municipal Statistics Bureau, 2011b). Accordingly, universities have to provide more space for the growing numbers of students. The new knowledge and technology has also brought demands for new facilities, which impose a construction burden on universities for additional space. Therefore, we see an obvious expansion of universities over the past decades.

Enlarging existing campus

Universities' built environment is often the result of decades, if not centuries, of planned or ad hoc change, balancing changing needs with available funds. Difficulties of university relocation exist in generating cost-recovery of initial heavy investment, agreeing commuting and other issues with staff and their unions, attracting students to the new campus, establishing positive relationships with the surrounding community and so on. So the university's first choice for expansion would be the place adjacent or near to the previous campus. This is a quite severe demand often involving the changing of urban land use structure, the relocation of residents from the university neighbourhood to new estates, the conversion of industrial, residential, commercial or other land to university uses, and the investment of huge amounts of money to get the land. And it is easier to exacerbate historic university–community conflicts due to their differences in terms of perception, values, goals, and available resources (Mayfield & Lucas, 2000).

A special aspect of university–community relations in China is embedded in the work unit tradition. As the carry-over from work unit organization, some neighbourhoods around the universities still remain as the living quarters of the university staff. It contributes to a shared public culture rooted in and shaped by the history and identity of the university, which makes it much more difficult to relocate residents due to their sense of belonging to the place, but at the same time also underpins a collective identity that provides a new possibility and sustainable way of integrating various stakeholders harmoniously into university spatial development. Take the outreach activity of Tongji University as an example: a commercial and business centre was planned to be developed around the university, which needed the neighbouring residential area of university staff to relocate. Most of the residents are well-known scholars who devoted themselves to the development of the university. They were reluctant to be relocated no matter how much compensation they could get. There was tough negotiation between the university and the community. What mattered at last was their shared culture and consensus for the good of the university: considering the future development of the university, the community finally agreed to move out to leave space for university expansion.

Building satellite campus

Considering the difficulty and cost of campus expansion in the inner city, most universities would like to develop satellite campuses in the suburb while keeping the main campus in the inner city, such as Jiading Campus of Tongji University and Fengxian Campus of East China University of Science and Technology. Usually, the satellite campus is relatively independent from the mother campus, with separate libraries, stadiums, students' residences and with commuting buses connecting to the mother campus. Taking Tongji University as an example, its farthest campus, Jiading Campus, is about 35 kilometres from the mother campus, which takes more than 40 minutes by car and more than two hours in public transportation. An affiliated administrative committee was set up in Jiading Campus to cope with daily management in a relatively independent way.

There are also some universities that relocated the whole or the main campus to the suburb, such as Shanghai Maritime University and Shanghai Ocean University from Yangpu District and Pudong New Area to Lingang New City. This is often because the requirement of university spatial development cannot be met in the original campus while the new one has a superb location, sufficient land, satisfying natural and social environment, and high quality teaching facilities. Most importantly, the funds for constructing the new campus can be partly financed through the expropriation of the original campus. In addition, urban and regional authorities who act as the original university landlords may see these assets as too valuable for educational use and prefer leaving the large urban site for upmarket housing and offices. At the same time, the relocation of the university may create opportunities for the vibrancy of the new nestle.

University towns

A strategic initiative led by local government to meet various challenges of university expansion is the setting up of university towns, which was very popular in many Chinese cities in the past decade. By April 2004, there had been 54 university towns newly established in 43 cities of China (Lu, 2005). Songjiang University Town, Nanhui University Town and Fengxian University Town were established successively in Shanghai. In addition, there are also some cases, mostly influential universities or university clusters, which have been planned to develop into a university town based on their existing spatial structures, such as Yangpu University Tow, which will be mentioned in Chapter 7.

The development of the university town is based on the principle of '1+1>2', which means that an extra value could be added and productivity gain could be achieved by gathering multiple universities together. University towns pull resources of those involved institutions together and make up one's disadvantages with the others' strength, while each institution remains relatively independent from each other. Colleagues and students joining the collaboration projects of these institutions can enjoy better resources such as excellent facilities and equipment for teaching, learning and research. It has effectively solved the challenges of university expansion and eased the tensions between urgent spatial needs of school buildings and rare economic value of urban lands. University towns perform as an efficient spatial form to facilitate cooperation between the universities and as an important catalyst for the fast development of the cities. They also help building an urban brand by profiling the city as a centre of excellence and making the city more attractive.

There are three types of university town considering their location in the city. The first type is strategically planned in the inner city on the basis of original concentration of universities, such as Yangpu University Town. They can make use of existing resources such as urban infrastructure, close university–industry linkages, and a favourable creative atmosphere. University towns of this kind usually develop faster, with less investment but better interaction with the city. The second type of university town is developed in the urban fringe with available cheap land and also convenient urban infrastructures and services. The third type is geographically independent from the mother city as a satellite town and is connected through a convenient transportation system. This kind of university town is usually on a large scale with extensive investment and long construction period. Most of the university towns in Shanghai follow the third model.

University engagement in urban spatial restructuring

In the process of university expansion, there has been constant interaction between the universities and the city. As the universities are increasingly engaged in urban development, the way that the campus is planned and built is changed accordingly. The campus plan no longer focuses on the self-containedness of the institution and its separateness, but performs as a key ingredient in the changing patterns of its neighbourhood, downtown, and city-wide development (Perry & Wiewel, 2005). A cluster of educational facilities that mix in seamlessly with commercial, retail, and service functions are major principles in the model of campus design. The university has become deeply involved in improving communities surrounding its campus by ensuring good schools, safe streets, good transportation, and attractive housing choices. The development of the multi-institutional and multi-functional campus often catalyses the deteriorated inner city and contributes to peri-urbanization. Through its own real estate development efforts, such as land clearance and infrastructure building, it is possible for the university to advance the overall citywide redevelopment and become the lead institution in this process.

For example, Shanghai Conservatory of Music and Shanghai Theatre Academy, in collaboration with Shanghai Library and Shanghai Audio and Video Archive, have enhanced the cultural atmosphere in the historical urban centre on the occasion of campus renewal. Shanghai Maritime University and Shanghai Ocean University have developed new campuses in Lingang industrial park, which is aimed to be a shipping centre by strengthening university–industry linkages: Shanghai Maritime University provides rent exemption to attract the world's leading shipping companies to establish an R&D centre, and Shanghai Ocean University embeds itself in the logistics, shipping, and marine industries to develop innovative fishery technologies. In Jiading District, the College of Automotive Engineering of Tongji University has attracted more than 800 billion yuan investment and developed into a large national innovation centre for automotive and rail technologies, which has promoted the urban brand of 'Automotive Jiading'. In Fengxian District, East China University of Science and Technology, Shanghai Normal University, and Shanghai Institute of Technology have tried to make use of their specializing disciplines and human resources to develop the district into a chemical industrial park as well as to explore the coastal tourism resources in the district.

Universities are natural catalysts of multi-nuclear sub-centres due to the concentration of university populations and infrastructures. Wujiaochang, one of the four sub-centres in Shanghai, for example, owes much of its prosperity to the agglomeration of universities. There are currently 14 higher education institutions around Wujiaochang, occupying 458.2 ha of land. The number of university students accounts for 40% of that in Shanghai. There are more than 500 research institutes and 40 national key disciplines in the district, respectively accounting for half of and two-thirds of the total in Shanghai. Nurtured by these universities, Wujiaochang has developed into a famous knowledge-intensive business district.

Universities also contribute to the formation of development zones. On the one hand, the increasing requirement for highly educated workers in the existing development zones requires the higher education services of universities. The high-tech jobs also encourage more collaboration between industry and the university. On the other hand, the knowledge-intensive nature of universities tends to invoke agglomeration of cultural industries and service industries, which lead to the specialization of the district into a development zone.

To integrate various university clusters into the urban plan, a '2+2+2+X' university spatial pattern was proposed in Shanghai. The first '2' refers to Yangpu Creative Cluster and Minhang Science Park led by key research universities; the second '2' refers to Songjiang University Town and Nanhui University Town with joint effort of the university, the government and enterprises; the third '2' refers to Fengxian University Town and Lingang Science Park that were newly developed for urban strategic integration and transformation; 'X' refers to a group of universities that have close linkages with innovative industries based on various disciplinary characteristics (Shanghai Municipal Education Commission, 2012). The '2+2+2+X' spatial restructuring involves numbers of universities, covers several urban districts, and integrates various sectors and institutions such as education, technology, economy, construction, finance, planning, transportation, real estate and so on. It takes into consideration the urban and the suburban as a whole in the planning process.

After years of exploration, a guiding principle of 'three-zone interaction' was put forward in Shanghai to maximize the role of the university in urban development. The three-zone refers to the university, the community and the enterprise. The three parts assume different roles in the process of university development. The universities function as the main source of knowledge production and personnel training, providing human resource and intellectual support for economic and social development. The community provides social services to universities and innovative clusters, aiming to create a favourable ecological and social environment. The enterprises facilitate the commercialization of academic research and management of industrial linkages, boosting innovative technology and its application into production. The role and power of different actors may vary across different stages and places of development. 'Three-zone interaction' is regarded as an effective and sustainable way of enhancing urban competitiveness by facilitating collaboration between the universities, the communities and enterprises in Shanghai.

The university 'of' the city versus the university 'in' the city

The close interconnection between the university and the city does not mean that their relations are harmonious and cordial. In fact, the relative independence of universities, especially those private institutions, creates potential urban criticism for their imperiousness and irresponsibility. University real estate practices, usually driven by the internal goals of campus design, academic program needs and endowment, easily exacerbate historic university–city conflicts and often run at odds with the broader urban and community development agendas of the city. For example, in the development of Jiangwan Campus of Fudan University, an expansion program occupying about 1 square kilometres of land, severe opposition was invoked from the communities against the large-scale land occupation of the university. In the past, it took about 15 minutes on foot or 5 minutes by bike for the communities to travel from their residence to the nearest metro station. After the setting up of the expanded campus, however, the communities have to circle around the campus, which increased both the time and financial cost. So they urged to open the university so that they can go through the campus along a shortcut.

As a product of its relationship with the city and its urban surroundings, the university is increasingly called for to be an urban university. An urban university is viewed to be 'of', not simply 'in', the city (Bender, 1988; Brockliss, 2000; Perry & Wiewel, 2005). It encourages teaching and research activities to address the specific problems and to meet the needs of society, integrates the teaching, research and service functions of the university across various disciplines, and promotes partnership between the university, government, industry and the community for the public interest (Mayfield, 2001). In general, an urban university is aimed to become a more vigorous partner in the search for answers to our most pressing social, civic, economic, and moral problems, and to affirm its historic commitment to the scholarship of engagement (Boyer, 1996).

An urban university operates with a closely meshed and intertwined mission, milieu, and environment. An operational definition of the urban university would incorporate both its setting and the clientele it serves. As suggested by the Coalition of Urban and Metropolitan Universities in the United States, several criteria apply to such institutions:

• location in a major metropolitan area
• dedication to achieving excellence through teaching, research, and public service
• a diverse student body reflecting the demographic composition of the region
• responsiveness and service to the local region as part of the university's mission
• serve the region not only by providing an educated citizenry and workforce, but also as a cultural and intellectual resource
• engage in partnerships with other local organizations
• use practical experience in the urban setting to enhance students' education.

At one time the term 'urban university' might be used only to describe institutions located in central cities, but this is no longer the case. Urban sprawl and the advent of 'edge cities' have changed the conventional notions of what constitutes urban. Today an urban university is one located in an urban agglomeration consisting of the densely populated urban core and its less-populated surrounding territories, irrespective of political boundaries or administrative definitions. An urban university can even be planned in a de-urbanized way, given the requirement of the urban plan. It can also shift locations between sites and even cities purposely in accordance with the urban strategy. In the development of satellite campuses, especially in the set up of university towns, the universities have been founded before significant urban development took place. Large-scale urban settlement came after the establishment of universities. The universities have led the suburbanization process of the city. It can be considered that the universities have been spilled out of the city deliberately to trigger large-scale urban development and to fulfil the strategic mission of the city.

While scholars are worrying about the university 'in' the city but not 'of' the city (Bender, 1988; Brockliss, 2000; Perry & Wiewel, 2005), new issues rise as the university is 'of' the city but not 'in' the city, which has made the university–city landscape more complex. Yet the question remains as to what extent the urban university, especially those universities 'of' the city but not 'in' the city, contributes to urban development. Depending on a university's location, in the centre of a large city, in a small town, an out-of-town campus or a completely disembodied virtual institution, the nature of such linkage and hence its overall impact vary. Compared with the suburb, urban locations provide a university with greater access, connections and linkage to the urban environment. Instead, the outflow of educational and cultural resources along with university suburbanization has undermined the intangible capital of the city not only due to the solely geographical retreat but also an overall capital loss due to the changing environment. Decisions on an urban university not to be 'in' the city should be given particular attention given its potential tremendous loss and gain to the city.

References

Bell, D. (1999). *The Coming of Post-Industrial Society: A Venture in Social Fore-casting*. New York: Basic Books.
Bender, T. (1988). *The University and the City*. Oxford: Oxford University Press.
Boyer, E. (1996). The scholarship of engagement. *Bulletin of the American Academy of Arts & Sciences, 1*(7), 11–20.
Brockliss, L. (2000). Gown and town: The university and the city in Europe, 1200–2000. *Minerva, 38*(2), 147–170.

Gu, F. R., & Tang, Z. (2002). Shanghai: Reconnecting to the Global Economy. In S. Sassen (Ed.), *Global Networks, Linked Cities*. New York: Routledge.

Li, Z., & Wu, F. (2006). Socioeconomic transformations in Shanghai (1990–2000): Policy impacts in global–national–local contexts. *Cities, 23*(4), 250–268.

Lu, B. (2005). *Researches on the Problems of Planning Construct and the Stratagem Adjustment on Present 'University City'*. (PhD), Southeast University, Nanjing, China.

Mayfield, L. (2001). Town and gown in America: Some historical and institutional issues of the engaged university. *Education for Health, 14*(14), 231–240.

Mayfield, L., & Lucas, E. P. (2000). Mutual awareness, mutual respect: The community and the university interact. *Cityscape, 5*(1), 173–184.

Perry, D., & Wiewel, W. (2005). From Campus to City: The University as Developer. In D. C. Perry & W. Wiewel (Eds.), *The University as Urban Developer: Case Studies and Analysis*. Armonk: M. E. Sharpe.

Shanghai Career Guidance Center for Graduates. (2001). *Conditions on Working in Shanghai for College Graduates Outside Shanghai Will be Significantly Adjusted in 2002*.

Shanghai Municipal Education Commission (Producer). (2012, 20 November). *Introduction of Higher Education in Shanghai*. Retrieved from www.shmec.gov.cn/web/concept/show_article.php?article_id=253.

Shanghai Municipal Statistics Bureau. (1991). *Shanghai Statistical Yearbook*.

Shanghai Municipal Statistics Bureau. (2001). *Shanghai Statistical Yearbook*.

Shanghai Municipal Statistics Bureau. (2011a). *Report No. 5 on 6th National Census: Steady Improvement of Population Cultural Quality, Urgent Needs to Strengthen Education and Training*.

Shanghai Municipal Statistics Bureau. (2011b). *Shanghai Statistical Yearbook*.

Tian, G. (1996). *Shanghai's Role in the Economic Development of China: Reform of Foreign Trade and Investment*. Westport: Praeger Publishers.

Wu, F. (2009). Globalization, the Changing State, and Local Governance in Shanghai. In X. Chen & Z. Zhou (Eds.), *Shanghai Rising: State Power and Local Transformations in a Global Megacity*. Minneapolis and London: University of Minnesota Press.

Wu, J. (2008). The peri-urbanisation of Shanghai: Planning, growth pattern and sustainable development. *Asia Pacific Viewpoint, 49*(2), 244–253.

Yusuf, S., & Wu, W. (1997). *The Dynamics of Urban Growth in Three Chinese Cities*. New York: Oxford University Press.

Zhang, Q. (2009). Technological progress and the transformation of economic growth pattern in Shanghai. *Contemporary Economics* (17), 92–95.

Zhou, Z., & Chen, X. (2009). Leaps and Lags in the Global Information Age: Shanghai's Telecom and Informational Development in Comparative Perspective. In X. Chen & Z. Zhou (Eds.), *Shanghai Rising: State Power and Local Transformations in a Global Megacity*. Minneapolis and London: University of Minnesota Press.

Part III

Case studies

6 A top-down strategy for urbanization
Songjiang University Town

Songjiang University Town is located in the southwest of Shanghai, about 30 kilometres from the city centre, and concentrates seven universities and colleges, namely Shanghai International Studies University, Shanghai Institute of Foreign Trade, Shanghai Institute of Visual Art, Shanghai Lixin University of Commerce, Donghua University, Shanghai University of Engineering Science, and East China University of Political Science and Law. It occupies an area of 5.2 square kilometres and is one of the largest university towns in China. The development of Songjiang University Town is a strategic initiative to meet the requirement of university expansion and to promote urbanization of Songjiang New City. It was led by Songjiang District Government and coordinated by Shanghai Municipal Government. Government-controlled enterprises were established to be responsible for real estate development around the university town. Other actors, such as banks and the peasant collective, were all involved in this process.

Urban strategies on the satellite city and university town set up

Songjiang used to be an agricultural county. In February 1998, it was authorized by the State Council to be an urban district and was planned to be 'a political and economic centre of the region, a historical and cultural town, and a relatively independent city in the southwest suburb of Shanghai' (Wang, 2001). At that time, Songjiang still performed as a centre at the county level. Its infrastructures and public services were provided just for the urban district and did not take into consideration the requirement of metropolitan Shanghai. Later, according to the master plan (1999–2020), Shanghai was aimed to become an international metropolis and China's economic, trade, financial and shipping centre, with a prosperous central city as well as competitive suburb. It was proposed to establish a multi-scale urban system including four levels of cities and towns – central city, new cities, central towns, and townships. The development priority was shifted from the urban to the suburb. As a consequence, Shanghai Municipal Government decided to select one new city and nine central towns as the key development nodes that could spread their influences to the surrounding rural areas. It was the so-called 'One City Nine Towns' strategy. The strategy was aimed to accelerate industrialization and urbanization in the suburb and to facilitate the industrial restructuring and urban transformation of central Shanghai. Fortunately, Songjiang was designated as the one new city.

The 'Great Leap Forward' of Songjiang New City was the set up of the university town. Songjiang had never been planned to be the agglomeration of universities according to the 'One City Nine Towns' strategy. However, its rapid development brought about considerable needs for human resources. As early as in 1995, government leaders had already been aware of the gap between the demand and supply of human resources in Songjiang (Yan, 2007). When Songjiang was selected as a new city in 1999, Songjiang District Government decided to attract one or two universities from other areas to locate in Songjiang and began to work hard for this. In 2000, along with the advancement of urban strategy in developing the city through science and education, Shanghai Municipal Government started to renovate the campus in the central city, according to which the universities in the central city would be relocated to the suburb in order to enlarge the campus and to improve the infrastructures. It provided a great opportunity for Songjiang to attract and host the universities.

The ultimate setting up of Songjiang University Town was attributed to both necessary and random factors. Some universities in the central city had to relocate to the suburb or build new campuses in the suburb to meet increasing enrolment requirements. It was necessary by any means. But with regard to where to move, it was random for any place in the suburb to host the new campuses. There are many factors influencing campus location, such as transportation, environment, infrastructure, opinions of the faculties, decisions of the university leaders and, most importantly, the land price of the new campus. Songjiang District Government would like to allocate about 3 square kilometres of land, valued at one billion yuan at that time, for free to the universities in order to attract them to settle down in Songjiang (Wang, 2001). This greatly delighted the universities because they did not need to be worried about substantive funding any more. Then Songjiang District Government signed contracts with Shanghai Municipal Education Commission in terms of the development of the university town and finished the construction of supporting infrastructures within half a year, which guaranteed the overall start up of the university town projects.

Songjiang University Town was planned as an integral whole and was constructed in two phases. The first phase included the campuses of the first four universities and was started in December 2000. It covered 2.7 square kilometres of land, on which was planned to accommodate nearly 1.2 million square metres of floor area. In October 2001, the first batch of 5,300 students began to move in, which attracted three more universities to join Songjiang University Town. In February 2002, Songjiang District Government signed another contract with Shanghai Municipal Education Commission and reallocated another 2 square kilometres of land to the north for the development of the second phase of Songjiang University Town. The second phase, which occupied 2.5 square kilometres of land and was planned to accommodate 1 million square metres of floor area, was soon put into construction. The first batch of 8,000 students from the latter three universities began to have lessons in Songjiang University Town in September 2003. The construction of the whole university town was concluded in 2005. The number of students in Songjiang University Town amounted to 72,000 in September 2007.

Governance coalitions in developing Songjiang University Town

Planning coalition involving multi-level governments and experts

As soon as the setting up of Songjiang New City was ascertained, Songjiang District Government organized a professional group, including both domestic and international experts, to prepare the outline of the master plan. The master plan was then submitted to Shanghai Municipal Government and finally approved by official decision. To prepare the detailed plan of various projects, a public tender was held in 2001. Five design studios from the United Kingdom (1), France (1), Italy (1) and China (2) were invited. Such an international tender of detailed planning on a piece of land with dozens of square kilometres rarely happened in China at that time, and there were neither related laws nor regulations to follow. The foreign studios were very excited about the tender but at the same time they were also worried about the evaluation process. Considering all these factors, the evaluation process was undertaken with strict rules: the planners and designers introduced their works; the international experts worked as judges and provided suggestions for further revision; counsellors from the three foreign countries were invited as witnesses; officials from Songjiang District Government and Shanghai Municipal Government censored the whole process. Finally, the superior ideas from different schemes were collected through public tender and worked as guidelines for the future development of Songjiang New City and Songjiang University Town.

Development coalition of governments and
state-owned enterprises

A development coalition including the governments, enterprises and universities was formed for the development of Songjiang University Town. Songjiang District Government provided the 5.2 square kilometres of land for free for the establishment of Songjiang University Town. However, it had to spend more than 1 billion yuan to expropriate the land use right, to relocate residents, and to compensate the landless peasants. Without any subsidy from the higher-level government, Songjiang District Government borrowed 1 billion yuan from the banks. A state-owned enterprise, Songjiang University Town Construction and Development Company, was then set up to carry out land development. It was entrusted by Songjiang District Government to participate in the primary land market, but it was strictly forbidden to be involved in any transaction in the secondary land market. Songjiang University Town Construction and Development Company was also responsible for the implementation of the university town planning, such as the construction of urban infrastructures, the improvement of the urban environment and the provision of public facilities.

Then, Songjiang District Government issued a series of favourable policies, such as tax reduction, to attract the enterprises to invest in the construction of the campus. Oriental Pearl Group, a state-owned cultural company, and several other enterprises got the development right. They formed the Construction Headquarter of Songjiang University Town with the coordination of Shanghai Education Infrastructure Centre, a sub-institute of Shanghai Municipal Education Commission. Thereafter, Shanghai Education Infrastructure Center, on behalf of the Construction Headquarter of Songjiang University Town, borrowed another 1.5 billion yuan from the Industrial and Commercial Bank for the construction of the university town. The enterprises of the Oriental Pearl Group and other investors have the ownership of Songjiang University Town. The universities rent the campus for a long tenure, using tuition fees and accommodation charges to pay the rent and management costs.

Management committee including municipal
government and universities

Songjiang University Town Management Committee is a branch office of Shanghai Municipal Education Commission. It is composed of the leaders of each university in Songjiang University Town and the officials of Shanghai Municipal Education Commission. Songjiang University Town Management Committee is responsible for coordinating the various activities of the universities such as resource sharing and socializing logistics. It is also entrusted by

Shanghai Municipal Education Commission to conduct administrative management and to supervise the daily operation of the university town. It consists of several offices in charge of student affairs, teaching and research, logistics services respectively. After the institutional reform in 2010, offices in Songjiang University Town Management Committee were restructured into different departments in charge of administration, investigation, public relations, and publicity. In addition, there is a student union under the leadership of Songjiang University Town Management Committee. It is constituted of student delegates from the seven universities in the university town and helps to exchange ideas between the universities and to organize cross-campus activities.

Service organization involving multiple sectors of the district government

Songjiang University Town Service Office was established by Songjiang District Government to provide public services and coordinate public affairs in the university town. It is a joint office consisting of officials from various bureaus of Songjiang District Government, including the Administration of Industry and Commerce, National and Local Tax Bureau, Health and Epidemic Prevention Station, Police of Urban Management and so on. They work together to check regularly the catering, lodging, entertainment and other public services in the university town.

Fantasy and reality in the planning of Songjiang University Town

Songjiang University Town takes sharing and interaction as the core value of a university town and has put much effort to promote their development. Songjiang University Town Management Committee was established to coordinate the sharing of educational resources and to promote higher efficiency of resource utilization. Teachers were encouraged to give classes across universities through employment contract; students were able to take lessons in other universities with recognizable credits. Public facilities in the university town were encouraged to open to all the students and faculties as well as to the neighbouring community. Logistics and daily services in the university town were no longer linked with any single university, but were operated by companies in the market.

The ideal of sharing and interaction was also vividly reflected in the spatial planning of Songjiang University Town. The central area along the longitudinal axis of the university town was planned to host the central library, gym, auditorium and theatre, which were shared by different universities. To facilitate frequent interaction among the universities, the students' living areas were separated from their own campuses and were concentrated along the horizontal axis of the university town. The walls between the different campuses were abolished to facilitate the flows of space and to encourage cross-border interaction inside the university town. The spaces with higher sharing potentials, such as the playground, were located at the periphery of the campuses so that they could be accessed easier by the other universities and the neighbouring community.

However, Songjiang University Town was not constructed according to the original plan, but was adjusted constantly in the implementation process. The contribution of public facilities to each university was considered unequal, especially in terms of distance, therefore unsuitable for frequent use. The universities also differentiate a lot in terms of size, type, discipline and so on, which cannot all be satisfied by the same standard. Therefore, the universities had to build their own public facilities to meet their particular needs. For example, both Shanghai International Studies University and Shanghai Institute of Foreign Trade built their own libraries, with 30,000 square metres and 28,000 square metres of floor area respectively, which have become their campus landmarks. The central library in the sharing space was finally cancelled since every university already had their own library. Although the central gym came into being in the end, it is not in efficient use because the universities have also built their own smaller ones. The sharing of public facilities exists just in name.

The integration of students' living areas was not realized as well. Although they were not enclosed by high walls, a two-metre high fence was used to separate the apartments of each university and there was a strict security check for visitors. This happened partly out of the consideration of safety because the neighbourhoods were under large-scale construction and there were frequent flows of people of various backgrounds. But it undoubtedly hampered free interaction between the universities and between the university and society. The ideals of Songjiang University Town – sharing and open interaction – did not come true in the implementation process.

In an investigation carried out by Yan (2007), 83.86% of the students considered sharing and interaction as an important factor influencing their choice when they decided to enrol in the universities of Songjiang University Town, and 52.33% of the respondents held the opinion that resources in the university town should be shared among the universities. However, 27.99% of the students in Songjiang University Town had never enjoyed the resources of other universities, 48.54% occasionally, and only 23.47% made frequent use. Concerning the role of Songjiang University Town Management Committee which was responsible for the coordination and daily management of the university town, although 98.43% of the students and faculties knew about its function, only 15.65% had some contact with it and only 12.11% would turn to it for consultancy and help.

Also, it was found that the attitudes of the universities towards sharing and interaction differentiated a lot. Shanghai Lixin University of Commerce, Shanghai Institute of Foreign Trade and Shanghai Institute of Visual Art showed higher interest towards sharing and interaction in the university town: the supportive ratio was up to 70%. In contrast, there were only 35% people favouring the idea of sharing and interaction in Shanghai International Studies University, Donghua University, and Shanghai University of Engineering Science. In general, the attitudes of different universities towards sharing and interaction were closely related with their own resources and competitiveness. For those universities with abundant resources and higher competitiveness, such as Shanghai International Studies University, they were not active to open and share with others. Instead, for those universities short of resources, such as Shanghai Lixin University of Commerce, they showed higher enthusiasm to support sharing and interaction.

Real estate booms around Songjiang University Town

The direct influence of Songjiang University Town was seen in the fast capital accumulation in Songjiang New City, which was reflected typically in increasing land price. Research showed that the influential area of the university town to real estate development was about 3–5 kilometres around (Lin, 2010). Before the development of Songjiang University Town, Songjiang New City was originally farmland and the land price was about 250,000 yuan per mu in 2000. After the set up of Songjiang University Town in 2003, land price in the south area of the university town rose to 360,000 yuan per mu, in the north to 400,000 yuan, in the west to 380,000 yuan, and the commercial area rose to 500,000 yuan per mu, double the previous land price (Li, Xiao, & Zeng, 2003).

The ninth metro line, which was put into use in 2007, has shortened the commuting time between Songjiang New City and central Shanghai from 2 hours to 35 minutes. It attracted more people to live nearby and thus raised the housing price. The housing price near to the ninth metro line is about 20% higher than other places in Songjiang New City. The average housing price in Songjiang District had increased about 2.5 times between the years 2000 and 2004 (Lu & Xu, 2006). Real estate investment in Songjiang District increased year by year and the annual rate of increase was up to 58% in 2005 (Table 6.1). The soaring land price soon recuperated the value of the land that Songjiang District Government had allocated to the university town for free, thus contributing to capital accumulation in the district.

The rapid development of Songjiang New City, however, had interrupted the regular rhythm of the real estate market and resulted in an imbalance between supply and demand. About 5.5% of the total area of Songjiang New City, i.e. 3.52 square kilometres of land, was put onto the market all

Table 6.1 Real estate investment in Songjiang District

	2003	2004	2005	2006	2007	2008	2009	2010	2011
Annual investment (billion yuan)	5.95	7.99	12.63	11.75	10.19	11.44	13.57	15.38	17.02
Increase over the previous year (%)	56.5	34.3	58.1	−7.0	−13.2	12.2	18.7	13.3	10.7

Source: (Songjiang District Statistics Bureau, 2004–2012); compiled by author.

of a sudden in 2003 (Songjiang District Statistics Bureau, 2004), contributing to a large quantity of commercial housing on the market in 2005. But the housing needs were not strong enough to absorb them all. Real estate development was at a too fast pace, which led to the oversupply and thus large-scale vacancy of the newly built housing. An investigation on the residential areas in Songjiang New City showed that about 16.4% of the newly built housing was left vacant (Tao & Lu, 2005).

Another factor contributing to the imbalance between supply and demand in the real estate market was the population structure. The population of Songjiang New City was planned to be 600,000 in 2020, but it was only 250,000 in 2007, among which 50,000 were students and staff of the university town, 25% were the elderly, aged 60 years and above, and the young, aged 15 years and below, and the rest were mainly concentrated on the periphery of the old town (Lu, 2007). Moreover, population growth in Songjiang New City was primarily due to migration of labours, students, house buyers and attracted talents. The number of each type of migrants was respectively 362,114, 51,175, 39,933, 1,108 in 2005 (Songjiang District Statistics Bureau, 2005). This kind of population structure made little contribution to the real estate market. However, the developers had ignored the population structure and focused exclusively on high-price large-area apartments. The area of most apartments in Songjiang New City was 100–140 square metres, the prices of which were 700,000 to 1 million yuan, whereas the small housing unit with about 90 square metres and at the price of 600,000 yuan was in short supply (Lu & Xu, 2006). Although the real estate market in Songjiang New City seemed over-developed, it still could not meet the needs of the residents. There was an imbalance between supply and demand in the real estate market.

University-triggered urbanization and industrialization

At the initial stage, public transportation between Songjiang and the inner city of Shanghai was scarce and it took about 2 hours by bus. The ninth metro line, a strategic public transport program connecting Songjiang with central Shanghai, had been planned to be finished in 2010. But due to the setting up of the university town, it was constructed ahead of schedule and finally put into use in 2007. Two public bus stations, Metro Station Transport Centre and Wenhui Road Transport Centre, were established by Sonjiang District Government around Songjiang University Town to extend transport from the metro station to the surrounding areas; some new bus lines were also opened. The improved transport system laid down the basis for urbanization in Songjiang.

The establishment of Songjiang University Town has transformed the land use structure in its surrounding areas. The previous agricultural land was gradually reallocated for industrial parks and commercial uses. Public institutes, such as the administrative body of Songjiang District, Shanghai First People's Hospital, and the branch of Shanghai Library were all settled down successively around Songjiang University Town. The 2.5 kilometre long street along the living area in the middle of the university town concentrates various services such as catering, publishing, telecommunication, bookstores, banks and so on and has become a famous commercial street in Songjiang New City. Investors in the commercial area to the south of the university town declared that 80% of their investment was oriented towards the consumption needs of the university town (Li et al., 2003).

Gradually, the employment structure in Songjiang was changed as well. The proportion of working population in the primary industry decreased from 17.0% in 2000 to 1.3% in 2010. In contrast, those in the secondary industry increased from 58.4% to 63.3%, and those in the tertiary industry increased from 24.6% to 35.4% (Songjiang District Statistics Bureau, 2011). As a consequence, the urbanization rate of Songjiang District increased dramatically. In 2000, there were only 254,500 people (39.7%) living in the urban area and 386,700 (60.3%) in the rural. In 2010, those living in the urban area of Songjiang District increased to 134,2900 (84.9%) and those in the rural decreased to 239,500 (15.1%). Comparing the population structure from the perspective of the urban household registration system, those with urban households in Songjiang District increased from 30.6% in 2000 to 81.7% in 2010, while those with rural households decreased from 69.4% to 18.3% (Songjiang District Statistics Bureau, 2011).

University towns and science parks often come up together. The abundant human resources in Songjiang University Town have stimulated the prospering of electronic industries. Taiwan Semiconductor Manufacturing Company, the leading company in the field of semiconductors in the world, was the first to develop its high-tech park on the west of Songjiang University Town. Later, the electronics and chip park invested by Acer of Taiwan was attracted to settle down in the northwest of Songjiang New City. The largest enterprises that have settled down in Songjiang Hi-Tech Park include Changjiang Computer Group Corporation and Shanghai Synchronization Electronics Company among others. The industrial structure of Songjiang District was shifted from dependence on light industry, textile, chemical, mechanical and instrumentation to the predominance of computer, electronics and other high-tech sectors. In 2011, there were 252 high-tech industrial enterprises with over 20 million yuan business income in Songjiang District, and their annual income amounted to 66.83 billion yuan in total, 8.1% higher than in 2010, whereas the annual income of all industrial enterprises with 20 million yuan in business income in Songjiang District had decreased 3.9% compared with 2010 (Songjiang District Statistics Bureau, 2012).

References

Li, C., Xiao, Q., & Zeng, G. (2003). Contribution of the Songjiang University–Town to the regional economic development in Shanghai. *Urban Research* (6), 73–76.

Lin, T. (2010). Suburban new town development and its impacts on the metropolis spatial structure: A case study of Songjiang, Shanghai. *Human Geography, 150*(8), 1056–1057.

Lu, J. (2007). Joint development of urban planning and real estate development: The case of Songjiang new city. *China Real Estate* (1), 65–67.

Lu, J., & Xu, Y. (2006). The influence of urban planning to the real estate market: The case of Songjiang University Town. *Real Estate Information of China* (11), 36–38.

Songjiang District Statistics Bureau. (2004). *Songjiang District Statistical Yearbook 2003*.

Songjiang District Statistics Bureau. (2004–2012). *Songjiang District Statistical Yearbook 2003–2011*.

Songjiang District Statistics Bureau. (2005). *Songjiang District Statistical Yearbook 2004*.

Songjiang District Statistics Bureau. (2011). *Analysis on the 6th National Census: The Characteristics and Influences of the Changing Population Structure in Songjiang District*.

Songjiang District Statistics Bureau. (2012). *Analysis on the Industrial Development in Songjiang in 2011*.

Tao, J., & Lu, F. (2005). *Optimizing Population Import through Industrial Upgrading*. In H. He (Ed.) *Almanac of Songjiang*. Shanghai: Chinese Dictionary Publishing House.

Wang, Z. (2001). The typical meaning of the advanced rapidly development of Songjiang new city, Shanghai. *Urban Planning Forum* (6), 12–15.

Yan, D. (2007). *A Study of Managerial Mode in University Towns: The Case of Songjiang University Town*. (Master), East China Normal University, Shanghai.

7 A bottom-up strategy for urban renewal

Tongji Creative Cluster

Tongji University, located in Yangpu District, in the northeast of Shanghai, has nearly 40,000 students and about 2,700 staff members. Among its various departments it is especially highly ranked in engineering: its architecture, urban planning, and civil engineering departments have consistently ranked first in China for decades. Tongji Creative Cluster was developed by harnessing the superiority of the university's leading disciplines in commercializing academic research and managing industrial linkages. It is the only national-level industrial park based on knowledge-intensive services in China. Different from the many science parks promoted by the government, Tongji Creative Cluster came into being spontaneously and grew up from the bottom. It was when the economic and social value of Tongji Creative Cluster was shown up that the governments began to intervene and provided financial and institutional support. Now, Tongji Creative Cluster has integrated driving forces of various kinds to promote its further development.

Spontaneous spatial spillovers of Tongji University

Tongji Creative Cluster is led by the architecture, engineering and construction sectors, whose ebb and flow is directly influenced by the real estate market. After China's reform and opening-up, especially after individual housing loans were released in the late 1990s, the real estate market began to prosper in China. There was a great demand in the real estate market driven by the long-term accumulated purchasing power and by the rapid urbanization process. But there was a short supply of human resources and public services in the fields of architecture design and civil engineering, constrained by the domination of a small number of state-owned enterprises. Along with economic reform in China, national control over the private economy was loosened and there were some preferential policies encouraging the development of small and medium private enterprises. This constitutes the external conditions for the emerging of university spin-off companies.

Institutional reform of the higher education system created the internal incentives for the development of Tongji Creative Cluster. After the reform, the modes of average distribution in universities were eliminated: personal income was largely dependent on the profit from research programs. This evoked the enthusiasm of professionals in applying their knowledge and research results for commercial use and building linkages with business communities. At the same time, Tongji University offered a tolerant environment for entrepreneurial activities: there was no restriction on the teachers' entrepreneurship or the students' part-time jobs; neither was there any regulation of those activities that undertake commercial programs by virtue of the university's brand. But the university charged a certain amount of money from the staff as a management fee. Usually it was 20% of the program funding. For those programs related to architecture design and urban planning, the fee amounted to 30%. In contrast, if the programs were carried out in an independent company, the total expense was no more than 10% (Liu, 2007). Therefore, most of the teachers and scholars were inclined to run business by themselves so as to maximize their benefit. The studios and research groups were gradually replaced by firms and enterprises.

As early as in the 1980s, some teachers and researchers began to set up companies publicly inside the university. Ancillary services such as rendering, model making and printing emerged subsequently. In the mid-1990s, along with the trend of university merger in China, Shanghai Institute of Urban Construction and Shanghai Institute of Building Materials were merged into Tongji University. And thus the number of enrolled students was largely increased. Facilities in the university, such as classrooms, dormitories and offices, were in serious shortage. Some functions had to be spilled out of the campus to leave space for expanded construction. The first to move were printing, model making and other supporting businesses; then the teachers' companies were moved out too. Most of them were relocated in the neighbourhoods along the adjacent Chifeng Road, a secondary urban street bisecting the university into a central campus and south campus. By 2003, there had been about 400 enterprises concentrated along the 860 metre long Chifeng Road, among which 47.13% were occupied in architecture-related jobs (Yu & Chen, 2005). The scenery of Chifeng Road was being transformed and it was gradually becoming famous for the agglomeration of design industries.

The prosperity around Chifeng Road attracted more companies and institutes to come. Graduates from Tongji University and designers from elsewhere began to set up companies around the area. They were settled in office buildings, storefronts, or the residential housing of the neighbourhoods. And this promoted the development of other neighbouring roads. Several well-known large design companies, such as Tongji Architectural

Design and Research Institute, Tongji Urban Planning and Design Institute, Shanghai Municipal Engineering Design & Research Institute, Lin Tung-Yen & Li Guo-Hao Consultants, were all attracted to settle there. By 2003, the cluster had expanded to 2.6 square kilometres around Tongji University, which formed the core area of the current Tongji Creative Cluster.

Government intervention in promoting Tongji Creative Cluster

Tongji Creative Cluster was originated from the spontaneous agglomeration of creative industries: there was no business tradition around the university, neither was there any public investment at the beginning. Moreover, dominant industries in Tongji Creative Cluster were neither high tech nor new science, which led to it being neglected by official urban plans. The government made little investment in Tongji Creative Cluster at the beginning stage, which however facilitated a tolerant environment for the cluster and alleviated its burden of investment returns (Pan & Lu, 2005). But along with its fast development, the social and economic effects of Tongji Creative Cluster were soon realized and the government began to intervene. The first to perceive the potential of Tongji Creative Cluster and to promote its development was Siping Street Office (Liu, 2007), a representative agency of Yangpu District Government. When Siping Street Office noticed the continuous rising spatial demand for offices around Tongji University, it proposed to transform the industrial plants in No.63 Chifeng Road into a creative park in collaboration with Tongji University. However, the proposal was rejected by Tongji University because of its worry about the market purpose of manipulating the university brand. Then Siping Street Office collaborated with Shanghai Institute of Fishery Machinery and Instrument and Hudong S&T Salon to undertake the program and achieved great success.

At the same time, economic development in Yangpu District, where Tongji University locates, was slowing down due to the stagnation of traditional industry. Yangpu District has been the traditional industrial base in Shanghai since the 1880s. Its industrial output amounted to 6.14 billion yuan in 1965, accounting for 26.52% of the total in Shanghai, and in 1990 it was 15.45 billion yuan, accounting for 14.59% (Office of Shanghai Local History, 2012). However, after China's reform of state-owned enterprises in the early 1990s, traditional industries such as textiles and manufacturing, which were characterized by extensive growth, could not adapt themselves well to the market mechanism and therefore met great challenges. The proportion of industrial added-value to the urban added-value in Yangpu District dropped from 34.24% in 1992 to 18.57% in 1998, and it ultimately became a burden for urban economic growth. It was necessary for Yangpu District to transform the modes of economic development. The prospering of Tongji Creative Cluster at that time provided such an opportunity and soon attracted the attention of Yangpu District Government.

In 2003, Yangpu District Government invested over 8 million yuan to improve the environment around Chifeng Road and officially named it Tongji Modern Architecture Design Street. When the enterprises along Chifeng Road were spilled out to the neighbouring area, Yangpu District Government invested another 5 million yuan to renovate the neighbourhoods and to acquire space for cluster expansion by exchanging land use right and reusing the idle buildings. There was a trend of developing university towns in China at the turn of the century and therefore the idea of Yangpu University Town was put forward by Yangpu District Government. The area around Tongji University and other neighbouring universities was planned as an integral part. It was aimed to facilitate collaborative growth through the joint effort of multiple universities and to develop the cluster into a high-tech industrial base predominated by large enterprises.

But it was soon discovered that the high-tech orientation of the cluster was in contradiction with Zhangjiang High-Tech Park, a national-level science park that was established in 1992. Based on the advantages of the university and the characteristics of the enterprises, Tongji Creative Cluster was readjusted to incubate small and medium start-ups based on creative industries, which could be integrated with Zhangjiang High-Tech Park when they developed onto a larger scale. A series of favourable policies and services were provided by Yangpu District Government. These included a financial service of preferential loans and venture investment for medium and small businesses, an entrepreneurship service of pioneering funding and guidance for start-up companies, a procedural service to assist program evaluation and funding application, a training service for policy interpretation and vocational training, a human resource service for personnel recruitment and recommendation, an intermediary service to provide professional consultancy about property rights, law, finance and so on.

In 2007, Wan Gang, the president of Tongji University at that time, proposed to develop the cluster around Tongji University into a knowledge economic area on the basis of Tongji Modern Architecture Design Street. The proposal received immediate approval from Yangpu District Government and they worked out together two important documents: 1) the Preliminary Agreement on Strengthening Further Cooperation in Promoting Independent Innovation, and 2) the Planning Framework for Tongji Knowledge Economic Area. The Cluster was planned to include the core area, the expansive area and a number of distant nodes (Yangpu District Government, 2011). The core area is centred on the main campus of Tongji

University, with an area of 2.6 square kilometres. The expansive area is a symmetrical pentagon surrounding the main campus, with an area of about 10 square kilometres. The distant nodes include several research institutes and science parks distributed in Yangpu District.

The cluster was formally launched by Yangpu District Government and Tongji University in May 2007 and was integrated into the management system of Zhangjiang High-Tech Park in 2008. In January 2009, the Cluster was included in the National Torch Plan by the Ministry of Science and Technology. It was the first and the only state-level industrial cluster characterized by knowledge-intensive services in China: all the other clusters in the National Torch Plan were based on high-tech industry. In September 2009, the Cluster was officially named the Tongji Creative Cluster by the Shanghai Economic and Information Technology Commission, and it ranked the first batch of Creative Cluster Exemplar in Shanghai in May 2010.

Self-reinforcement of Tongji Creative Cluster

Tongji Creative Cluster enjoys some critical attributes of self-reinforcement. Spatial networks due to high density and mixed use in the Cluster contribute to frequent interaction and entrustment among the various actors; business networks help to reduce the transaction cost and unite the enterprises of various kinds to jointly resist market instability; the continuous moving in and out of intellectuals and enterprises keeps fresh momentum in the Cluster and contributes to its self-renewal.

Spatial networks

Due to the long-term inefficacy of public capital at the initial stage of Tongji Creative Cluster, most real estates in the Cluster were subject to private control. It was difficult to implement large-scale demolition and construction. Corresponding measures such as zoning to purify land use cannot prevail in the Cluster either. The upgrading and renewal of the physical facilities in the Cluster were carried out in an incremental and flexible manner, such as reuse, multi-use and mixed-use, which contributed to the spatial complexity in the Cluster. For example, the industrial plants of Shanghai Institute of Fishery Machinery and Instrument in Chifeng Road No. 63 were reconstructed into a creative park in 2001 through the joint effort of Hudong S&T Salon, Siping Street Office, and Shanghai Institute of Fishery Machinery and Instrument, providing 41,869.5 square metres of space for creative companies; the residential housing of Shuxiang Apartment and Guokang Apartment around Tongji University were largely rented for commercial and office uses. Different functions are concentrated in the same building. Some even share the same office.

Spatial proximity is beneficial for enterprises to reduce transaction costs, especially transportation costs, which is of particular importance for small businesses with a limited budget. So the cluster predominated by small enterprises tends to have higher density and more efficient use of space. The closer to the core area of the Cluster, the higher density and the more efficient use of space there is. It was estimated that over 90% of office buildings in the core area of Tongji Creative Cluster were occupied (Pan & Lu, 2005). Taking an office building on Chifeng Road as an example, the floor area of the building is 2,500 square metres, and there settled as many as 11 enterprises. The direct and close spatial connection among enterprises helps to frequent contact and corresponding entrustment. Some enterprises have established contractual and long-term business relationships based on their spatial connection. Spatial networks contribute to social networks in the Cluster, and vice versa social networks contribute to spatial agglomeration.

Business networks

Tongji Creative Cluster is overwhelmingly predominated by small companies. In 2004, the average number of employees in the companies of Tongji Creative Cluster was fewer than 16; in 2008, the number rose to 25, but there were still 78.3% of the enterprises with fewer than 20 people (Q. Chen & Wang, 2010). Without complex internal functions, small and medium enterprises depend more on externalities and industrial chains. Tongji Creative Cluster is in high degree of labour division and an integral industrial chain has been formed involving the design industry at the core, design-oriented services such as handicrafts and the software industry as the second layer, business administration and the information industry as the third layer, and public services such as goods delivery, real-estate brokerage, equipment maintenance, travel agencies, banks and restaurants as the outer layer (Yangpu District Government, 2011). There are professional and specialized companies involved in every section of the industrial chain. The industrial chain contributes to a favourable environment that greatly reduces the transaction cost. It is estimated that the cost to set up a design company in Shanghai is about 1 million yuan, disregarding the daily expense and registration fees to run business. But in Tongji Creative Cluster it costs only 150,000 yuan to set up a design company (Pan & Lu, 2005). The lower investment to run a company reflects the advantage of Tongji Creative Cluster to attract start-ups and small enterprises, which also explains well its continuous vitality.

Settlement of several large enterprises in Tongji Creative Cluster is also an indispensable factor for the success of the Cluster. In China, there are different requirements for the qualification of participants to take part in different projects, defined by professional and technical credits. Most small enterprises in Tongji Creative Cluster do not have the required qualification. In addition, it is usually difficult for small enterprises to undertake complex projects by themselves due to their relatively inferior professional techniques. When applying for projects that require high-level techniques, they have to cooperate with the large enterprises and 'borrow' their qualifications. On the other side, large enterprises are sometimes too busy to be engaged in all projects, but they are not willing to lose customers, so they would like to sub-contract some projects to small enterprises. This kind of sub-contracting is of mutual benefit for both large and small enterprises and it creates abundant entrepreneurship opportunities for young designers, which contributes to the prosperity of Tongji Creative Cluster. In fact, most of the business that small enterprises undertake originate from their cooperation with the four large enterprises in Tongji Creative Cluster. However, such a business network, dependent on sub-contracting, is very unstable. The small enterprises tend to close down whenever there is any shrinkage in the market. But, on the other hand, it helps to the self-renewal of Tongji Creative Cluster, with those less competitive easily washed out.

Self-renewal

Pan and Lu (2005) carried out a survey on the location choice of enterprises in Tongji Creative Cluster and they found that the highest scored factors influencing location choice were 'adjacency to university', 'concentration of peers', 'place brand' and 'sensitive to new ideas'. These factors were nearly the same as the satisfactory factors of Tongji Creative Cluster evaluated by the enterprises. It showed that Tongji Creative Cluster has some attributes as expected and valued by the enterprises, which explains well the reason for its attractiveness. Among all the enterprises in Tongji Creative Cluster, nearly half of them were opened in other areas first but then were attracted to move into Tongji Creative Cluster (Q. Chen & Wang, 2010).

Many enterprises in Tongji Creative Cluster are evolved from research groups in Tongji University. The organization of research groups extends out of the university, which forms a 'club' linking groups of alumni firms with potential partners. It is estimated that 80% of the enterprises in Tongji Creative Cluster are set up by alumni of Tongji University (Liu, 2007). Teachers and researchers work as professional consultants in the Cluster or set up companies by themselves. Some projects undertaken in the Cluster are often selected as teaching cases in university courses. The students of Tongji University participate often in the projects with guidance from the teachers or do internships and part-time jobs directly in the neighbouring enterprises. Investigations showed that 42.9% of the students in Tongji University have the experience of doing part-time jobs in Tongji Creative Cluster, of which 53.6% are involved in programs related to their majors (B. Chen, Liu, Fan, & Peng, 2006). They perform as low-cost and high-quality temporary employees for Tongji Creative Cluster. What the students have gained in this process, such as professional experience, entrepreneurship knowledge, project management skills, market awareness and social capital, lays a solid basis for their future career, which may end up as skilled personnel in Tongji Creative Cluster.

While there are continuous new start-ups and inflowing enterprises in Tongji Creative Cluster, many enterprises that were originated and incubated in Tongji Creative Cluster have already grown out of the Cluster and are integrated into other high-tech parks in Shanghai. Tongji Innova Engineering & Technology Company, for example, the first professional auto design and engineering company in China, was founded in Tongji Creative Cluster in 1999. Now its design capability and enterprise scale is ranking first in Asia and third in the world. It set up an R&D centre in Jinqiao Development Zone in 2002 and another one in Nanhui Development Zone in 2005. Many other enterprises that were born in Tongji Creative Cluster have also been scattered around Lujiazui, the Bund, People's Square and other sub-centres in Shanghai. Tongji Creative Cluster is not only attracting many enterprises in, but also sending some out, which keeps fresh momentum and helps to its self-renewal.

Flexible driving forces in the development of Tongji Creative Cluster

In the development process of Tongji Creative Cluster, there are various driving forces. One usually serves as a motive force, around which the others revolve. Their relations are rarely stable but tend to change at different stages and in different circumstances. It is the flexibility embedded in the development strategy that enables Tongji Creative Cluster to be easily adaptive to the complex social environment and to be competitive in the market.

Different stages, different driving forces

There are different driving forces at different development stages of Tongji Creative Cluster. At the initial stage, it was driven by the spontaneous spill-over effect of university spin-off companies, which owed largely to the institutional reform of the university. When the Cluster began to grow, the neighbouring community, which was led by Siping Street Office, played an important role. The community had a strong desire to encourage the agglomeration of creative industries and to promote the development of a creative cluster. Although their initial proposal to develop a creative park in Chifeng Road No. 31 did not get any support from Tongji University, their effort to meet the increasing spatial needs of housing and offices was critical for the growing of Tongji Creative Cluster. Along with the urban strategy of relying on science and education for economic restructuring, Tongji Creative Cluster got special attention from Yangpu District Government and Shanghai Municipal Government, with financial and institutional support that led to the rapid expansion of the Cluster.

When the market value of Tongji Creative Cluster was shown up, real estate developers engaged to make large investment in commercial projects, which helped to maintain a superior environment for the Cluster. For example, Tongji Yangpu Science and Technology Venture Development Company carried out market research on Tongji Creative Cluster and found that office space was in serious shortage whereas the entrepreneurial trend was still prevailing and small start-ups continued to emerge. It proposed to establish Shanghai International Design Center and got immediate approval from Yangpu District Government. Tongji Yangpu Science and Technology Venture Development Company then purchased land use right in the environs of Tongji University with the coordination of the government, and invited several large enterprises such as Shanghai Design Institute of Posts and Telecommunications and Tadao Ando Design Company to settle there. Meanwhile, it invested 9 million yuan to improve the environment. During this process, Tongji Yangpu Science and Technology Venture Development Company enjoyed some preferential policies as part of the national science park and transformed from a purely commercial developer to a quasi-public institute.

Different places, different driving forces

The driving forces of Tongji Creative Cluster also differentiate across places, such as the two creative hubs around Chifeng Road and Guokang Road. Chifeng Hub was originated from spontaneous agglomeration of design companies around the university; whereas Guokang Hub was developed through strategic planning in response to the rapid expansion of creative industries. They were driven by different forces at the initial stage of their development. Although after several years both of them have incorporated forces of various kinds, there is still a great difference in terms of the power of the forces. It is this difference that leads to further diversity in

Table 7.1 Comparison of the development modes between Chifeng Hub and Guokang Hub

	Chifeng Hub	Guokang Hub
Location	Urban street, easy accessibility	Urban island, limited accessibility
Origin	Spontaneous agglomeration	Official planning for cluster expansion Real estate development
Previous Land Use Structure	Mixed-use, private real estate, high density, high complexity	Industrial plants of state-owned enterprises
Land Development	Exchange land use right Incremental, step by step	Expropriate land use right and reallocate Large-scale reconstruction
Management	Self-regulation according to market laws	Government-led property company
Industrial Structure	Private medium and small enterprises Sufficient auxiliary services Interdependent	State-owned or university-affiliated large enterprises Insufficient auxiliary services Self-dependent

Source: made by author.

their development strategy and management modes (Table 7.1). In Chifeng Hub, government intervention is constrained by the complexity of spatial structure and the diversity of property rights, so its development is proceeding step by step with incremental adjustment, predominated by market mechanism and self-regulation. In contrast, Guokang Hub used to be the industrial plants of state-owned enterprises whose land use rights are easily expropriated and then reallocated through government intervention, so its development is prone to large-scale reconstruction and subject to the management of government-controlled property companies.

University engagement in urban renewal

Tongji Creative Cluster has proved to be an effective catalyst for local development, particularly for the transformation of Yangpu District from an old industrial base to a knowledge economy centre. Geographically, Tongji Creative Cluster helped to improve the neighbouring environment and to optimize the land use structure. Economically, an integral industrial chain was formed in Tongji Creative Cluster, contributing to the local tax and employment positions. Institutionally, successful experiences in Tongji Creative Cluster have been fixed as official strategies to maintain the long-term viability and to set an exemplar for other cases.

Geographical

Yangpu District is an old industrial district. Its industrial land was about 12.8 square kilometres at the end of 1998, accounting for 21.3% of the total (Li & Chen, 2005). Along with the shift of urban strategy from Industrial Yangpu to Knowledge Yangpu, it was necessary to relocate industrial land out of the central city and to provide more space for university expansion and creative industries. By expropriating and reallocating land use rights on the occasion of university engagement activities, Yangpu District Government managed to coordinate the spatial demand of different actors and to optimize the urban land use structure. For example, Yangpu District Government expropriated the land use right of Shanghai No.1 Bus Company and reallocated it to the adjacent Tongji University, so that Tongji University can transfer its land use right in Wuchuan Campus to the neighbouring Shanghai University of Finance and Economics. In this way, the parking house of Shanghai Bus No.1 Company, occupying about 80,000 square metres of land, was redeveloped as a design centre to meet the increasing spatial need of Tongji Creative Cluster; and, at the same time, Shanghai University of Finance and Economics got sufficient space from the neighbouring area for campus expansion. In another case, two plots amounting to about 400,000 square metres of land from Shanghai Bicycle Factory and Shanghai Construction Machinery Factory were reconstructed as student apartments for Fudan University and Shanghai University of Finance and Economics. Some other science parks in Tongji Creative Cluster, such as No.63 Chifeng Road and Shanghai International Design Center in Guokang Road, were all developed on the basis of the renovation of industrial plants. A large amount of industrial land was put into efficient use after the government's expropriation and reallocation.

Economic

The development of Tongji Creative Cluster has made great economic contribution to Yangpu District and even the whole city. Its output value kept increasing at the rate of over 20% every year, with 7.98 billion yuan in 2007, 10.2 billion yuan in 2008, and 12.3 billion yuan in 2009 (Yuan & Zhao, 2011). During the 11th Five-Year Plan period (from 2006 to 2010), the number of enterprises in Tongji Creative Cluster had increased from 227 to 800, their floor area had almost doubled, the number of employees had increased by more than four times, and the output value increased by more than 5.5 times. The tax from Tongji Creative Cluster at the district level amounted to 208 million yuan in 2006 and increased to 504 million yuan in 2010 (Yangpu District Government, 2011). Driven by Tongji Creative

Cluster, modern design industries have been playing a more important role for the economic development of Yangpu District. Their output value increased from 4.92 billion yuan in 2006 to 10.24 billion yuan in 2010 and contributed 434 million yuan to district tax revenue in 2010. The added-value of knowledge-based services and high-tech industries in Yangpu District reached 14.88 billion yuan and 2.94 billion yuan respectively in 2011, with the former paying 1.60 billion yuan and the latter 0.24 billion yuan tax to the district government.

Institutional

At present, there is multi-level interaction among the university, government, industry, the community, developers and other actors involved in Tongji Creative Cluster. At the decision-making level, senior leaders from Tongji University and Yangpu District Government constitute a joint committee to discuss the strategic plan and major issues concerning the Cluster development. At the implementation level, representatives from the university, government, the enterprises and specialized experts participate in the project altogether to guarantee the interests of the various actors. At the communication level, there is an agreement of exchange and cooperation: scholars from the university are invited to work in the government, and officials from the government are sent to the university for further education. Positive social relations are established through frequent interaction, which contributes to the establishment of various partnerships. Some successful experiences in the development of Tongji Creative Cluster have already been institutionalized and spread to other areas of the city. The strategy of three-zone interaction, mentioned in Chapter 5, for example, was first created in Tongji Creative Cluster on the basis of positive interaction between the university, the community and enterprise, and was later adopted by the municipal government as an exemplar.

References

Chen, B., Liu, T., Fan, J., & Peng, K. (2006). The study on the interrelationship between human resources and urban space in districts with a high-density of intelligence – Taking Yangpu district as an example. *Urban Planning Forum* (3), 9–15.

Chen, Q., & Wang, L. (2010). Cultivation system of cluster of knowledge-intensive service industry. *Forum on Science & Technology in China*.

Li, D., & Chen, B. (2005). The strategy of the re-use of the old industry land in the Yangpu old industry area: From industry Yangpu to knowledge Yangpu. *Urban Planning Forum* (1), 44–50.

Liu, Q. (2007). *The Research on the Creative Cluster Development Surrounding University in Urban Renewal*. (PhD), Tongji University, Shanghai.

Office of Shanghai Local History. (2012). *Industrial History of Yangpu District.*

Pan, H., & Lu, Y. (2005). The positive research on the form reason and construction of the enterprises around the university: Take the example of the enterprise community surrounding Tongji University. *Urban Planning Forum* (5), 44–50.

Yangpu District Government. (2011). *12th Five Year Plan for Knowledge Economy Cluster around Tongji.*

Yu, D., & Chen, B. (2005). Study on the effect of social capital on the concentration of knowledge-based industries: A case of areas around Tongji University. *Urban Planning Forum* (3), 64–70.

Yuan, S., & Zhao, X. (2011). A study on government role in the formation process of industrial belt around university: Based on the analysis of 'Tongji phenomenon'. *Science & Technology Progress & Policy, 28*(19), 57–60.

Conclusion

The purpose of this book is to explore changing university–city relations in the knowledge society from a spatial perspective. By analyzing the conditions, actions/interactions, and consequences of university spatial development at the global, national and local levels, it tries to understand the dynamics of university–city interaction in the knowledge society. This chapter provides a conclusive review on the research results. First, it explains the dynamics of university spatial development and urban transformation and the mechanism of their interrelations in the knowledge society. Next, it identifies the tensions and barriers to university–city interaction. Finally, it proposes spatial strategies for mutually beneficial university–city relations.

Dynamics of university spatial development and urban transformation

In this book, analysis on the dynamics of university spatial development and urban transformation in the knowledge society is guided by a multiscale coding matrix. In the following, we will summarize the findings about the dynamics at various levels according to the basic components, i.e. the conditions, actions/interactions and consequences, of the coding paradigm, which are also corresponding to the sub-research questions: what are the social and urban contexts for university spatial development, how is the space of the university developed, and how is the city transformed due to university spatial development.

Social and urban contexts for university spatial development

Cities today are caught up in a globalizing world as a result of the technological revolution and capitalism restructuring in which economic, technological, political and cultural features are intertwined (Kellner, 2002). But neither capitalism nor technical innovations are new; both are common and recurrent phenomena through the ages. What is brand new is their speed of diffusion and their global reach across culture, classes and geography (Drucker, 1993). The speed and scope are driven by a radical change in the meaning of knowledge: knowledge is fast becoming the basic means of production, side-lining natural resources, labour and capital. The central wealth-creating activities in the global system are shifted from the allocation of capital and labour for productive uses to 'productivity' and 'innovation' through applications of knowledge. Intangible capital, which includes human resources and institutional quality, has become a key factor in determining global urban competitiveness. As a response, cities have to embrace learning as an urban strategy to be successful in the global competition. Learning makes it possible for cities to assimilate the incredible amount of new knowledge that they regularly produce and to make full use of the networked relations that they are indulged in. The capability of universities to facilitate learning has become an important measure for the transformative power of a learning city.

Cities today are also experiencing a fundamental change in the philosophy of governance and the way the public sector is managed. The mode of governance associated with the classic ideal type of bureaucracy is in the process of being deconstructed. In its place are emerging forms of governance that bring both state and non-state actors into the policy process. In China, for example, the central state has since the late 1970s abandoned direct allocation of production materials, capital, land and workforce, transferring the power and responsibility to the local level and at the same introducing market mechanisms in the provision of public services. Cities get more power and autonomy in making decisions on local affairs and become strategic arenas of state governance. Promotional measures such as development zones, infrastructure improvement, prestige projects and land markets, have been adopted by cities to attract foreign and private investment. Therefore we have seen fast urban development in China during the past decades. As urban development began to take hold, it was soon discovered that the labour quality and the educational qualification of workers in China was too inferior to keep up with the fast development of the urban economy. Out of these issues began a process of higher education reform to meet rising market demand.

As China's leading metropolis, Shanghai has been undergoing dramatic socio-economic restructuring since the 1990s. The tertiary industry has increased substantially and has overtaken the secondary industry to become the largest. Producer services such as finance, insurance and real estate constitute the leading edge of the growth of tertiary sectors. Industries with advanced technology increased while traditional light industries decreased. It shows that urban development in Shanghai is in transition from factor-driven and investment-driven to innovation-driven. Thus higher education has become a lever of economic growth. To transform into a 'first-rate' international metropolis with the best talents, Shanghai Municipal Government has promulgated a series of policies to allow selective social groups with higher education to work and live in Shanghai. Correspondingly, in the rapidly enlarging occupation sectors and upgrading income levels, there is a trend of progressively improving educational attainment. The relationship between education and income has become stronger, with an increasing influence of human capital and entrepreneurial activity on earnings. Unemployment happens mainly to those low-skilled and middle-aged workers with poor education. People with higher education have seen large increases in productivity and pay. Therefore higher education has become a promoter of social mobility.

The actions and interactions in the process of university spatial development

As a kind of important knowledge infrastructure of learning cities, universities are offering flexible and innovative responses to the rapidly changing economies. A remarkably diversified organization of universities that transcends the conceptual, institutional and geographical boundaries of traditional universities has created new opportunities to meet the growing social demand, such as virtual universities, franchise universities, corporate universities, mobile universities and academic brokers. The diversified and flexible forms in the organization of university, coupled with the growing demand for international sharing of education and training, have transformed the global geography of urban universities: international education mobility has become more frequent due to the advancement of technology; cross-border campuses are facilitated by national policies with the expectation of entry into the global market; university cooperation and alliances are established to attain goals beyond the reach of any single university; global universities are strategically concentrated in global cities to maximize their benefit. The historic alignment between the city and the university is giving way to one based more on global networks.

In the Chinese context, the localization of universities in cities began with the national policy of restructuring higher education governance. To fit universities better to local development, the leadership of some universities originally led by different central ministries in China has been transferred to local governments, while others are under joint development of central and local government. The local governments place the universities under local economic and social development plans and provide investment funds for them; in return, the universities gear to the need of local economic and social development in their enrolment criteria, curriculum design, graduate employment, scientific research and so on. At the same time, to align higher education with fast urban development, universities are incorporated into the national innovation system and are encouraged to strengthen the combination of education, scientific research and social application. Selective universities can receive substantial funding from central government to expand their research capacities and disciplines, with matching funds from local governments. University–industry partnerships are developed through principal–agent relationships, spin-off companies, or collaborative programs. Some enterprises are even directly run by universities to facilitate the engagement of universities in S&T activities.

As the universities are increasingly involved in urban development, the way that the campus is planned and built is changed accordingly. Campus plans no longer focus on the self-containedness of the institution and its separateness; a cluster of educational facilities that mix in seamlessly with commercial, retail, and service functions are major principles in the model of campus design or expansion. These university-affiliated mixed-use campus developments are not simply real estate ventures. They embody a commitment of the universities to partake in broader activities, offering companies high-value sites for accessing researchers, specialized facilities and students, and promoting live–work–play environments. Science parks – a geographical concentration of interconnected companies, specialized suppliers, service providers, universities and associated institutions in particular fields that compete but also cooperate – come into being either spontaneously or with official promotion, which has provided a sound environment for innovation ranging from managing real estate to fundraising, from talent hunting to assuring legal arrangements.

Any spatial development is not an easy matter for universities because it usually involves the changing of urban land use structure, the relocation of residents from the university neighbourhood to new estates, the conversion of industrial, residential, commercial or other land to university uses, the investment of huge amounts of money to get the land, and so on. It is easier to exacerbate historic university–community conflicts due to their differences in terms of perception, values, goals, and available resources (Mayfield & Lucas, 2000). To avoid the difficulty and to reduce the cost of campus expansion in the inner city, some universities would like to develop satellite campuses in the suburb. The new campuses help to create opportunities for the vibrancy of the new nestle. A strategic initiative led by local government in China to meet the various challenges of university expansion is the setting up of university towns. University towns pull resources of those involved institutions together and make up the one's disadvantages with the others' strength. It has effectively solved the problems facing universities in terms of limited space for school buildings, and thus eased the tension between university expansion and rare urban space.

Urban transformation due to university spatial development

Rather than being necessarily structural followers of urban transformation, universities have often successfully transformed the way of urban development. University expansion has provided more opportunities for higher education and promoted the accumulation of human capital for urban development. Networks among universities generate an entry for cities into the global/regional circuits and are relevant to the trade dimension of international higher education services as well as other related interests. It is also an alternative way for cities to develop academic excellence without heavy investment in and long-term commitment to the creation of large university establishments. The strategic localization of the universities is not only aimed to seek consistency with the local environment, whether market, infrastructure, or culture/society, but also in a way that is consistent with the university's strategy and operations in other places of the world. The local environment may have to be inventively moulded if the university organization and strategy in one city are not to become inconsistent with those in other cities.

To maintain an advanced and superior environment, pro-growth coalitions are formed with the joint effort of the university, government, industry, and other related important actors. They are represented by a number of hybrid organizations on the basis of entrepreneurship, such as collaborative programs and joint ventures. The coalition based on entrepreneurship is not permanent and stable; it is focused on the priority of projects. Those projects that can suit the needs of the market, such as science parks, are especially supported. Those of less profit but of public good may be left behind. The strategies of the coalitions are adjusted constantly according to the particular requirements of the projects, inducing institutional ambiguity from time to time. On the part of the Chinese state, these hybrid organizations and ambiguous institutions are deliberate to allow experimentation and prevent social upheaval given that institutional ambiguity can serve a protective function. But it also increases cognitive uncertainty and risks by providing socially irrationalized rules for action, such as a grey land market and triangular debt.

Supported by the development coalitions, universities have emerged as key ingredients in the changing patterns of neighbourhood, downtown, and citywide development. University areas are a natural catalyst of sub-centres due to the concentration of the university population and resources. The knowledge-intensive nature of universities tends to invoke agglomeration of cultural industries and service industries, which lead to the specialization of the district and contribute to the establishment of development zones. The development of mixed-use campuses often catalyzes the deteriorated inner city and contributes to peri-urbanization. The location of an urban university is strategically manipulated between locations, sites and even cities according to the urban strategies. Through its own real estate development efforts such as land clearance and infrastructure building, it is possible for the university to advance the overall citywide redevelopment and become the lead institution in this process.

Tensions of university–city interaction

The dynamic interaction between universities and cities does not mean that their relations are always harmonious and cordial. In fact, there are often tensions and conflicts. Some are of long-term existence right from the beginning while some emerge in the new situation. Corresponding to the nature of the space of the university as a social product, tensions exist in the urban universities' spatial orientation and practices, the relations and orders established in the process, and underlying culturally embedded symbols and values.

Challenges to the paradigm of urban university

New situations have brought about new challenges to the so-called 'urban' university. The universities are leaving their historical rooted cities along with the development of cross-border campuses and suburban sites. The development of satellite campuses, especially cross-border campuses, creates reciprocal attraction between the university and the city. The university is looking for an attractive city to locate itself in order to attract more talent. And the city is also looking for competitive universities to promote its competence by virtue of university resources. In a world of global networks, both universities and cities need to identify their own space to survive in their mutual selection. Moreover, with the emergence of the virtual university, the original reason that brought students to be physically close to their teachers no longer pertains (Brockliss, 2000). In a world of new technology, both the university and the city also need to identify what will be the essential cement maintaining their interconnection in the twenty-first century.

At the same time, suburbanization of the universities has happened in many cities along with the process of urbanization and university expansion. It has indeed eased the tension between university expansion and rare urban space and has promoted the fast development of the suburb. However, compared with their urban congeners, suburban universities have limited interaction with the city. They are alienated from the urban community due to long distance, and they are often enclosed by walls due to safety considerations, which has definitely isolated them from the surrounding suburban areas. Suburbanization has downgraded the social attributes of the universities. Moreover, along with the suburban development of universities, educational and cultural resources have flowed out of the city. It has undermined the intangible capital of the city not only due to the solely geographical retreat of the universities but also an overall capital loss due to the changing environment. Suburbanization of the universities is a two-edged sword to urban development.

Conflicts between the stakeholders

In the process of university spatial development, there are many interest groups involved – students, academicians, companies, the neighbourhood, government, developers et al. They all have a stake, something to gain or lose as a result of the university's spatial activities. Although collaboration among stakeholders can be mutually beneficial, there are usually conflicts between them. The relative independence of universities, especially the private institutions, created potential urban criticism for their imperiousness and irresponsibility. University real estate practices, usually driven by internal goals of campus design and academic program needs, easily exacerbate historic university–city conflicts and often run at odds with the broader urban and community development agendas of the city (Perry & Wiewel, 2005).

It has been found that the conflicts between universities and communities are often not caused by the instrumental results but rather the problematic social relations among partnership members (Prins, 2005). For example, failing to specify partnership purposes, membership, and expectations regarding decision-making and authority increases the risk of confusion and disputes. Often, disputes are not about the issue at hand but rather about what it represents, such as the experience of disrespect or the illegitimate exercise of authority. The relationships among stakeholders are subtle and complicated. They are affected in various ways by actions, decisions, policies, practices or goals both in and beyond the process of university spatial development. The specific interests that different stakeholders have may be partially contrasting. The role of universities to affect local development depends crucially on their ability to balance the multiple relationships established between the place in question and its stakeholders (Russo, Berg, & Lavanga, 2007).

Moreover, the global visions and ambitions of the universities often run in contradiction with the local agenda. As universities grow in importance as part of the knowledge economy, their power and need for autonomy will grow. However, the growing importance of universities also exerts a greater incentive for the cities to maintain their control. Therefore, the reduced public subsidy into higher education is shifted toward particular private interests that are beneficial to the state (Rhoades & Slaughter, 2006); the government is less favourable toward those public research whose outcomes are open to all and for everyone's free benefit, especially when the resulting innovations are easily captured by foreign companies and the local economy gets zip (Marginson, 2010). By controlling the finance and shaping the new knowledge, local government exerts influence on the global agenda of the university.

On the other side, local authorities may have unrealistic ambitions for what universities can achieve as urban development policies in the knowledge economy are characterized by a huge amount of me-too-ism (Benneworth, Charles, & Madanipour, 2010). Many local authorities idealize new university developments as being necessary to trigger fundamental urban transformation, e.g. promoting the city into the global circuits. However, the reality is that many regions worldwide do not host a Stanford University or MIT. The universities may have local benefits, but do not substantially improve that locality's global positioning. The establishment of science parks may have substantially improved the economic performance of the industrial sectors rather than promoting a world-leading innovative cluster as centres of the knowledge economy.

Confusion about the role of university

Today the space of university is developed to achieve many goals that used to be predominated by other institutions, such as economic momentum by industrial and commercial sectors, social services by public agencies and global orientation by multinational corporations. A new model, which is strategically planned mixed-use campus design, is emerging and involves seamless coexistence of educational, commercial, retail and service functions. Meanwhile, in a knowledge-based society, every institution is attempting to harness knowledge and intelligence at all points of its organizational and management systems. Learning groups of various sizes are encouraged, formally and informally, ranging from networks of shared interest to corporate universities and science parks and then to learning cities. The distinction of the space of university is challenged, which causes reflection on the nature of the university. Actually, the anxiety is not about the engagement of the university per se; it is the elimination of any clear boundary separating university from other urban institutions (Washburn, 2005).

The engagement of the university in so many areas also generates doubt about its effectiveness. Investigations in America found that only a few universities make significant profits from technology licensing; many others barely break even – or even lose money (Washburn, 2005). Similar results are also found in Chinese universities: about 40% of university enterprises in China were involved in S&T related activities in 2001 and their sales revenue made up a mere 2.3% of all high-tech enterprises nationwide (Xue, 2006). It is evident that the universities' commercial interventions are only slightly successful. To what extent universities contribute to the socio-economic development of their urban hinterland remains a questionable issue. Therefore the orientation of university spatial development for commercial uses should also be managed carefully.

In addition, along with the role of university being elevated to an equivalent status as government and industry, the notion of Triple Helix is regarded as a guiding principle in dealing with university–government–industry relations. However, the ideal model of Triple Helix does not apply to all the cities, given their divergence in terms of development stages, historical university–city relations and so on. Even though there is a pursuit of Triple Helix in theory, it is difficult to fulfil in practice. In Shanghai, for example, the municipal government proposed 'Three-Zone Interaction' as the guiding principle in university spatial development, but the reality is that government has always become the leading force no matter in a top-down or bottom-up manner. This necessitates the diversified modes of innovation, which remains to be discovered. Perhaps, in the Chinese context, it is better to be defined as a government-led innovation model rather than a Statist Model in the past or Triple Helix in the ideal. That is to say, there is still constant interaction between the university, government and industry, but government is always playing a leading role to determine the final direction of innovation.

Spatial strategies for mutually beneficial university–city relations

The last part of the book tries to give some recommendations on how to better manipulate university–city relations in the knowledge society. It is oriented towards the general world situation while also pointing out some particularity of Chinese cases. The spatial strategies are proposed in response to the tensions discussed above, thus penetrating into the three levels of the social formation of the space of university – the spatial practices, social interactive processes and underpinning ideologies.

Aligning university spatial development with the changing social environment

The rise of the knowledge society and the consequent necessity of learning in urban strategy imply that the university can no longer be confined to a set and settled space–time. To effectively support the intellectual requirements of the city, universities have to incorporate flexible methods in the organization of space. Virtual universities, franchise universities, mobile universities and corporate universities are all new variants of the traditional campus-based university. Meanwhile, the university should encourage cross-border mobility and international cooperation, which would be an effective supplement to the permanent sources of funding and hierarchical organizational patterns. For those cities lacking investment in higher education, building networks will be an alternative way of enhancing self-capacity with less cost. Universities should also build networks with other knowledge producers and users, since knowledge production in the global era is no longer proceeding in a hierarchical way but is socially interactive.

When we do not know the outcome of our actions, we cannot develop grand plans. Instead, there should be small and step-by-step changes. Universities occupy a large quantity of land and buildings; the adjustment of these properties by the universities will generate profound consequences for their host cities. Therefore university spatial development should follow a step-by-step evolutionary process and proceed by trial and error, with frequent mid-course corrections and reversals of policy. For example, in the gradual development of Tongji Creative Cluster, its strategy was able to be adjusted in time to avoid competition with Zhangjiang Hi-tech Park, which has got strong national and local support in the same field. Successes or failures in some universities can also work as a reference for others. In this sense, the reform experience in China provides a good example for other countries and cities.

Establishing long-term partnerships between stakeholders

University–city coalitions can address urban problems better or more cost-efficiently than acting alone. Coalitions can be developed on the basis of hybrid organizations, which assume a broad range of forms and sizes, both formally and informally, such as cooperative agreements, collaborative projects and joint ventures. There can be temporary university–city coalitions on the basis of entrepreneurship, which provide practical and specific responses to particular program issues. But, more importantly, there should be permanent and stable university–city coalitions that can avoid speculation and protect public interest in the process of university spatial development.

To maintain the long-term viability of university–city coalitions, it is necessary not only to make internal institutional changes of either partner, but also to institutionalize it at the national and local level (Legates & Robinson, 1998). Internal institutionalization of the universities and the cities will benefit from inter-university or inter-city organizations that share relevant information, create and disseminate national models, organize training sessions, facilitate personnel decisions both formally and informally, develop standards, and other advancement in their particular domain. Institutionalization at the local level involves not only achieving a stable and long-term university–city coalition or even successful creation of a university–city decision-making structure based on specific circumstances and characters of either partner, but also developing working relationship with the local counterparts of the upper-level stakeholder groups such as transnational corporations and foundations. Institutionalization at the national level includes assuring continued favourable policies for collaboration, joint action among multi-level government, participation of multiple stakeholders in the resolution of spatial issues, and part independence of the university to avoid becoming passive arms of certain group.

To effect enduring changes in urban transformation, university spatial development needs to penetrate underlying culturally embedded assumptions and habits. There should be a cultural approach and more balanced policies to overcome the growing disparities among diverse actors in university spatial development. For the university, culture serves a particular unifying function by constituting national culture and producing good citizens (Readings, 1996). The transition from elite university to mass university enables a shift in the university from a high-cultural role to a broader cultural role (Chatterton, 2000), which is helpful to promote a progressive, open and tolerant culture (Florida, 2002). In particular, the work unit tradition in Chinese universities would be of strategic importance to ease the tension between the university and the community. It is based on a shared public culture rooted in and shaped by the history and identity of the university, and is helpful to facilitate a collective identity, providing a possible and sustainable way of integrating various stakeholders harmoniously.

Keeping a systematic perspective on the role of university

University by itself does not transform cities, nor is there any guarantee of positive returns on investments in the space or in other properties of universities. Many cities have invested heavily in building up university real estate without reaping significant returns. This is because space yields its greatest value when it is embedded within a positive and appropriate social environment. To maximize the benefit of university spatial development, it is necessary to link the space of university with the knowledge society, to incorporate university spatial development within a complex system of institutions and practices known as the innovation system. An innovation system is a web made up of the knowledge-producing organizations, the appropriate macroeconomic and regulatory framework, innovative firms and networks of enterprises, adequate communication infrastructures, and other factors such as access to the global knowledge base and certain market conditions that favour innovation (World Bank, 1999). Any progress in urban innovation is far beyond the spatial practices of any single institution. Although universities figure prominently in this framework, serving not only as the backbone for high-level skills but also as a network base for information sharing, the effectiveness of its innovative role and any positive outcomes of related spatial practices depends crucially on the promotion of such an innovation system.

The space of university is often managed to promote the third mission of the university, which includes several different activities such as the commercialization of academic knowledge through collaboration with industry, patenting/licensing, creation of spin-off companies, participation in policy-making, involvement in social and cultural life. All these activities are strongly related to and based on the missions of teaching and research. The stronger that is education and research, the better the third mission can be developed. In contrast, the university will lose its essential and valuable asset in serving society without teaching and research. While the university spatial development supporting the third mission is highlighted in the process of adapting to new challenges, those spatial practices contributing to the first and second mission should also be strengthened instead of ignored, even though they do not yield instant and direct economic benefit.

References

Benneworth, P., Charles, D., & Madanipour, A. (2010). Building localized interactions between universities and cities through university spatial development. *European Planning Studies, 18*(10), 1611–1629.

Brockliss, L. (2000). Gown and town: The university and the city in Europe, 1200–2000. *Minerva, 38*(2), 147–170.

Chatterton, P. (2000). The cultural role of universities in the community: Revisiting the university–community debate. *Environment & Planning A, 32*(1), 165–181.

Drucker, P. (1993). *Post-Capitalist Society.* New York: Harper Business.

Florida, R. (2002). *The Rise of the Creative Class.* New York: Basic Books.

Kellner, D. (2002). Theorizing globalization. *Sociological Theory, 20*(3), 285–305.

Legates, R. T., & Robinson, G. (1998). Institutionalizing university–community partnerships. *Journal of Planning Education & Research, 17*(4), 312–322.

Marginson, B. S. (2010). The Rise of the Global University: 5 New Tensions. *Chronicle of Higher Education.*

Mayfield, L., & Lucas, E. P. (2000). Mutual awareness, mutual respect: The community and the university interact. *Cityscape, 5*(1), 173–184.

Perry, D., & Wiewel, W. (Eds.). (2005). *The University as Urban Developer: Case Studies and Analysis.* Armonk: M. E. Sharpe.

Prins, E. (2005). Framing a conflict in a community-university partnership. *Journal of Planning Education & Research, 25*(1), 57–74.

Readings, B. (1996). *The University in Ruins.* Cambridge: Harvard University Press.

Rhoades, G., & Slaughter, S. (2006). Academic Capitalism and the New Economy: Privatization as Shifting the Target of Public Subsidy in Higher Education. In R. A. Rhoads & C. A. Torres (Eds.), *The University, State, and Market: The Political Economy of Globalization in the Americas.* Stanford: Stanford University Press.

Russo, A. P., Berg, L. V. D., & Lavanga, M. (2007). Toward a sustainable relationship between city and university a stakeholdership approach. *Journal of Planning Education & Research, 27*(2), 199–216.

Washburn, J. (2005). *University Inc.: The Corporate Corruption of American Higher Education.* New York: Basic Books.

World Bank. (1999). *World Development Report 1998/1999: Knowledge for Development.* New York: Oxford University Press.

Xue, L. (2006). *Universities in China's National Innovation System.* Paper presented at the UNESCO Forum on Higher Education, Research and Knowledge, Paris, France.

Index

For Product Safety Concerns and Information please contact our EU
representative GPSR@taylorandfrancis.com
Taylor & Francis Verlag GmbH, Kaufingerstraße 24, 80331 München, Germany

www.ingramcontent.com/pod-product-compliance
Ingram Content Group UK Ltd.
Pitfield, Milton Keynes, MK11 3LW, UK
UKHW021423080625
459435UK00011B/140